ACS

TRADITION AND EXPERIMENT
IN PRESENT-DAY LITERATURE

TRADITION AND EXPERIMENT

IN PRESENT-DAY LITERATURE

ADDRESSES DELIVERED
AT THE CITY LITERARY
INSTITUTE

London. City literary institute.

1929
OXFORD UNIVERSITY PRESS
LONDON : HUMPHREY MILFORD

OXFORD UNIVERSITY PRESS
AMEN HOUSE, E.C. 4
LONDON EDINBURGH GLASGOW
LEIPZIG NEW YORK TORONTO
MELBOURNE CAPETOWN BOMBAY
CALCUTTA MADRAS SHANGHAI
HUMPHREY MILFORD
PUBLISHER TO THE
UNIVERSITY

Printed in Great Britain

PREFATORY NOTE

THESE lectures were delivered in London during the Lent Term, 1929, at the City Literary Institute. They formed one of the short courses which are there arranged from time to time, additional to the ordinary work of the Institute, to give opportunity to the students to hear as many as possible of our most distinguished writers, and to discuss with them such problems as may arise from the lectures. The thanks of the Institute are due to the speakers for the freedom and goodwill with which they have taken part in the discussions, and for the mental excitement which they provoked and perhaps even shared. By their courtesy also it has been possible to bring their lectures into a book which, it is hoped, will prove as definite a contribution to contemporary criticism as the lectures themselves were to the intellectual experience of the hearers.

T. G. WILLIAMS
Principal.

CONTENTS

TRADITION IN THE NOVEL

R. H. MOTTRAM

I AM deputed to try to throw some light on Tradition in the English Novel. I must begin by making clear what I mean by the title under which I speak.

The general tradition in the English novel, as in anything else that is English, is to have no strongly marked tradition. It is part of the genius of these islands that colonels should look and behave like squires, stockbrokers like colonels, and novelists like anything except devotees of a literary tradition.

It would hardly be too much to say that the tradition of the English novel is experiment. Here I must stop, lest I trespass upon ground reserved to others who are to speak to you, only reminding you that, as English-speaking people, you cannot be too careful about the real meaning—the historic meaning—of the words you use. If you are careful you will be able to make fewer words suffice, and this, we know, is the soul of wit. The danger that you may not be careful arises from two interconnected facts—one is the relatively large size of the English vocabulary, and the other the lack of any official control. Were you, for instance, French people, you would have to be more exact in your speech and thought, and you would be made more exact by the fact that there is in France an official body, so to speak, in charge of the language. Such is the general atmosphere in which the English novel has arisen.

The series of which this lecture forms a part deals specifically with modern literature. I, however, hold very strongly to the fact of continuity in all expressions

B

whatever of the human spirit. I cannot possibly segre-gate that which is precisely modern, and above all, in surveying tradition, I may have to take you back over a rather lengthy period. Tradition is, of course, that which is handed down through, or more exactly across, the ages with their varying historical incident. Let us see from what the English novel derives.

The novel is most usually defined as an imaginative presentation in prose form of life. This is a wide definition, but we can narrow it, by considering what prose forms we habitually exclude when we think of the novel.

The present form of the novel, like so much of the exterior form of the amenities of an advanced civiliza-tion such as ours, is very largely dictated by convenience. You will find it very difficult to get a novel published in England unless it is between sixty and a hundred thousand words, and unless it is sufficiently entertaining to pass attractively the leisure moments of the modern town worker. That is the brutal fact about the modern novel. It can hardly be called a vehicle of entertain-ment, but rather one of distraction. It answers thus to the environment we have, with so much trouble and sacrifice, disposed about ourselves. Most of us who practise the writing of it cannot produce the ideal marketable article. We are preoccupied with trying to create what is, to us, a work of art. This accounts for the fact that you are sometimes told that only 2 per cent. of the manuscripts submitted are published.

The modern novelist is like a man shooting at a target that isn't there, or is, at any rate, invisible. Only when the constant shifting of the most ephemeral part of the public taste in entertainment happens to bring the target into line with the shot fired, do you hear of a great novel. You must not confuse a great novel with 'the latest success' nor yet with one of those lonely masterpieces that are so called because no one can understand or assimilate them. There is still, one hopes, sufficient conscience in the novelist and sufficient discrimination in the public to ensure that some novels worth reading are widely read. Such is the present situation. How has the English novel arrived there?

You will notice that I am incapable of dealing with the novel as though it were some recondite literary form existing only in the world of art. To me, the novel is not only a literary form, but an article of merchandise and an item in the well-estimated family budget, where it figures under the heading of 'amusements'. In other words, it belongs essentially to the modern world of commerce, and as we have already seen, of convenience. This cuts it off from every other literary form. Poetry not only has behind it an exaltation of spirit that is mainly foreign, and not in the least necessary to the novel, but has always been called forth by an utterly different demand. The Epic began as a rhymed chronicle and survives as a sort of literary equivalent of commemorative sculpture; Drama derives from religious ritual and calls into play other faculties than those we employ in the appreciation of the novel. The Lyric is still, at its best, what its name says it is, a sublimated song, and bears traces of having had an instrumental accompaniment. The earliest prose that I know anything of is historical or didactic. All this is easy enough. Our difficulty is in defining the tradition of the English novel. Stories, usually in groups, and with little or no historical and didactic impulse, made their first appear-

ance in England—I mean England and not Great
Britain—through the foreign influence of the Renaissance. I am thinking of course of Chaucer.

Have we then, in Chaucer, the beginnings of the
tradition of the English novel? Obviously not. The
English novel, as it exists to-day, is generally considered
to have begun with Richardson's *Pamela* and *Clarissa
Harlowe*. Can we connect this name with Chaucer's?
We cannot. Yet the fact remains, that if we accept the
definition of the novel as an imaginative presentation of
life, there is a relationship between the *Canterbury Tales*
and the novel, in the fact that the predominant motive
in both is the entertainment of persons of leisure.
Nearer than that, the two do not come. I do not think
we can put the name Tradition to a similarity between
two forms which are separated by such a formidable
gap. It is a gap that has more than one dimension.
First of all there is the gap of time. The story as such
did not so much disappear as find itself crowded out by
the splendour of succeeding Drama and Lyric. Prose,
in fact or in intention, was written, but chiefly for
other purposes than stories. If the Elizabethan wanted
entertainment he had the Drama or the Lyric. But
the Elizabethan was followed by the Jacobean, and the
Jacobean by the Caroline, and the Caroline by the
crucial last decade of the seventeenth century which
marks the beginning of modern England.. In that
decade Richardson was born. He was the first to write
what we nowadays call a novel and nothing else. I am
quite aware that others—notably Defoe—had written
or were writing what we should also call novels or
novelettes. But these books—*Robinson Crusoe* and others
—were largely side-lines of authors who were deeply

immersed in the drama, in politics, or in other interests.
Richardson, so far as I know, wrote to amuse and certainly expected to be paid for it. He did not spend years
in exile on account of his opinions. He was a citizen
of commercial London. He was no Bohemian, could
practise and certainly had practised a trade, and was a
married man with a large family.

If you accept Richardson as the father of the tradition
we are discussing, we may stop to glance at the gap, in
another dimension, that makes me so sure that there is
no descent from ancient story-telling to the novel. This
becomes visible when we reflect that the short story
came, late in the nineteenth century, to have a vogue
of its own—that it has maintained its position now, for
roughly half a century—as a literary form competing
with, and perfectly distinct from, the novel. I am not
concerned at the moment to argue as to the tradition
of the short story. Its only importance to me is the
vagueness of the distinction between it and the novel.
This would not matter so much if the short story had
not come into such close and confusing favour, along-
side the novel, so that, although less common than in
some continental literary schools, it is still possible, in
England, to find a writer of big reputation such as
Mr. Kipling spending nearly all his literary career in
writing short stories, and only once using the novel
form. And if you can tell me why you always describe,
as I am sure you do, *The Light that Failed* as a novel,
and nearly all of the author's other books as collections
of short stories, you would get as near as I can take
you to defining the novel. I should be most interested
to know how you describe *Kim* and *Captains Courageous*.
If they are not novels, what are they? Not short stories

certainly. I will suggest to you that they miss being novels by the fact that their heroes are children, and their matter narratives of events rather than plots based on interaction of character. This leads us back very conveniently to the early eighteenth century. One of our difficulties in making Samuel Richardson the father of the novel, is the fact that *Pamela* appeared after Defoe had published *Robinson Crusoe*. Why, then, do we not take Defoe as the novel's progenitor, and *Robinson Crusoe* as its first example? The reason is the same as that which I have suggested in the case of *Kim*, neither book contains exactly what we mean by the word novel. That is to say, our prose 'imaginative presentation of life' is divided into two forms of distinct scope and nature. There is another material distinction which you will appreciate if you have had anything to do with the actual writing, printing, and publishing of books. You will find that however misty may be the dividing line between the novel, the short story, and the narrative of adventure, the book trade has no such incompetencies. Editors and publishers will tell you plainly enough that a short story must be extraordinarily good if it is to exceed 30,000 words, that a full-length novel must contain at least 60,000, and that the other is in the category 'Juvenile Department'. Let us therefore thank God for editors and publishers, who keep us in touch with the solid earth, and prevent us from flying off into some horrid sectarian Nirvana of Art with a Drawl.

Now what did Mr. Samuel Richardson of Salisbury Court, Fleet Street, do to make himself so eminent? He did not write extremely good novels, in fact I fancy most of you will find them trying to read. They were, however, new, just as Richardson himself was new.

He arrived in the world just too late to be governed
by a King by Divine right, or to live in an England
restored to the hegemony of Catholic Europe, as
James II would have liked to restore her. Richardson
was one of the first modern Englishmen, a tradesman of
London, the capital of the vaguely Protestant limited
monarchy that we know to-day. Only a generation or
two earlier the people of England, and especially of
London, were entertained by drama which cast a halo
of magnificent rhetoric over sordid murder or obscure
legend, or by lyrics which placed the kissing of a
scullery-maid in the kitchen on a level with the ravish-
ment of Helen of Troy. Richardson was modern in
that to him a sordid story was sordid, a seduction a sin.
In fact, Professor Saintsbury says that the moralist is
stronger than the story-teller in Richardson. There was
not much else in him, no great beauty of style or depth
of sympathy, but he did reduce romance to a manage-
able proportion in the form that he was perhaps the
first to use, and which we call the novel. Romance
remained in the fact that his stories were imaginative,
not legendary, historical, or biographical, and like all
true Englishmen, he was a snob, which means a weak
and mundane type of romanticist. He always gave his
humblest character some aristocratic connexion.

Contemporary with him, more or less, came Defoe,
Fielding, Smollett, Sterne, who took on the novel and
did something distinctive with it. And I want you to
notice once more that none of them were mere story-
tellers. They were all of them wielders of satire—a use
of prose canonized by the genius of Swift, to name
no others—either on political or moral grounds, and
generally on both. They were, if one may risk an

analogy with another art—Hogarthian. And they all substituted for the romance of the anaemic-grown, conventional, classical fable, the robust adventure narrative that they related to, but did not copy from, personal experience.

In them, I think you may see the tradition of the novel fixed. What a composite, English structure it was! Upon a backbone of selected veritable incident, arranged so as to form the life-story, or part life-story, of the hero—nearly all their titles are male names—they hung both the invective that another tradition—the parliamentary and legal one—has ousted from our legislature and law courts, and the aspiration that had been confined to poetry. This backbone, or plot, was articulated by life-like character drawing, and, with few exceptions, convincing dialogue and apposite description. For adornment, they used the rough out-door humour of the time, and never forgot the pathos that touches the susceptible emotions of the Englishman. Thus every sort of taste was catered for, and it is not surprising that the royalties paid to this group of un-conscious and mainly unrelated pioneers were high then, in comparison with the rewards obtained by the older arts, and would be considered handsome nowa-days. I mention this because that sort of encourage-ment is important in favouring the establishment of a tradition. Had the novel been neglected and poorly paid, it might never have survived, for it cannot be written under the pressure of some spiritual exaltation, as one would like to think good poetry is—it is too large and has no rigid metrical frame to stiffen it. It suffered, then, from at least three sorts of competition which did not affect it again until our own post-war period, if

then. Oratory was a great art and an important factor
in life. The theatre was very popular—but above all,
sermons and pamphlets were bought and read, as they
continued to be down to the time of our own grand-
parents, who used to give each other books of sermons
for birthday presents. The novel maintained itself and
that is why it has survived.

The great men whose names I have mentioned, who
made Richardson's discovery accessible and practicable,
were all dead when the eighteenth century had run a
little more than half its course. The novelists who fill
the rest of the century belong rather to my colleague who
is to deal with experiment. No great development of
tradition occurs until the epoch of the Napoleonic War
brings us to Scott and Jane Austen.

The development they show is so striking that we
must see it as a reaction to the general trend of our
national history. The Revolution which had deprived
Samuel Richardson of the glamour of the seventeenth
century left the beastliness and the corruption of the
eighteenth uncovered. I do not say that this century
was really worse than the preceding one, I say that it
was more naked. That is why, in spite of the admiration
you cannot but feel when you read the great novelists of
the period, you cannot but be revolted by the state of
society they portray. That state of society was producing its own natural revulsion. The practical, un-
philosophic English sense of decency and order in the
home and the street was asserting itself. Or, to look at
the matter from the strictly literary standpoint, you
will find that Professor Saintsbury describes what happened as the triumph of Romance. Now the faculty of
romance is simply that of being able to see human

nature as rather better than it ever was or could be. You may be sure that no medieval baron or highland chieftain was ever so clean-mouthed or so easily upset by moral considerations as are those you meet in the Waverley Novels. The shocked propriety of Rebecca and Amy Robsart never protected any living woman's virtue, nor did the originals of Brian de Bois-Guilbert or Leicester ever bottle up their passions to the point of dying of emotional combustion. In Scott, then, you have romanticized historical incident, touched with the necessary pathos and humour to hold an immense audience. His great advantage, apart from natural gifts and a remarkable industry, was the fact that hardly a period in which his stories are set comes within half a century of his own time, and there is no view to which distance lends such enchantment as that of human nature. But the case of Miss Austen is far more remarkable. Her novels were written and published while Britain was in the throes of a struggle as vital as that of 1914–18. You would never guess it from her plots, which usually turn upon the one and only final love affair of the young lady of the period, which invariably led to her betrothal to the young gentleman of whom she was the choice. The life depicted is the contemporary life of hall and rectory, of birth, death, and marriage, of Bath and Bloomsbury, of parties, or morning service, and visits to the seaside. I am not belittling Jane Austen, I am marvelling at her. With no historic panoply to aid, she used the romantic faculty so delicately as to make English upper middle-class life interesting. The effort was well worth it. That life is still the most civilized and desirable in the world.

Scott and Jane Austen have a high proportion of the

romantic and a low one of the didactic ingredients that
go to make the English novel. The reason that the
proportion was altered if not reversed in Charles
Dickens must be found in the impalpable nature of
romance. It is impossible to live in the clouds, even
the solid feather-bed-like clouds as they appear when
viewed historically or from within the comfortable
middle classes. Dickens was a member of that poor
suburban clerkdom which we know to be numerically
more characteristic of British life than the dominant
upper middle classes.

Although employing the romantic faculty to the
verge of the fantastic, Dickens could not prevent from
sticking through it the bones and sores of starved ill-
treated bodies that formed the cannon—or rather
factory—fodder of the phase of the industrial era, let
loose by his post-war period. With all his romantic
vitality, his humour, his pathos, his subject-matter
conscripted him into the ranks of the satirists. He was,
for all his extravagances, a great confirmer of the tradition of the English novel. Its backbone of personal
life, or part-life narrative, already fixed for him by his
predecessors, he finally sealed with two elements that
the English novel is never likely to escape, and which
are most characteristic, I mean the love interest and
the happy ending. Nothing would have so astonished
an Athenian or a medieval public. Nothing so completely satisfied the deepest longings of Victorian
Britain. The thing which makes me so sure that this
is in the direct descent of tradition, is the fact that
Dickens has gone down into the heart of the people, as
no other printed word has, except the Bible. How often
have we not seen those 'Symposiums on the World's

Best Books' and 'My Favourite Author'? Does not the
Bible come first, and Dickens or some of his works next,
with *Robinson Crusoe* and then probably *Uncle Tom's
Cabin*? Dickens had also characteristically the vitality
and industry of Scott. He fills the tradition to its outer
edges. He used the short story considerably and gave
readings of a sort that make him nearly an actor. In
fact I should be interested to know whether you can
call the *Pickwick Papers* a novel, without qualms, and
whether you do not feel that Little Nell, Paul Dombey,
and Tiny Tim do not belong rather to the theatre than
to literature. And always remember that Dickens did
not invent, he illumined.

After having said this, it is difficult to pass on to
Thackeray without seeming to disparage. I do not
mean to do so, and there is certainly in Thackeray a
keener sense of style, and a greater avoidance of
buffoonery. It always seems to me, however, that
Thackeray's is a less complete picture of English life,
certainly he has never laid hold of English people as
did his great contemporary. Music-hall impersonators
still 'do' Dickens's characters to audiences who do not
miss the allusion. They never put on Thackeray's. Nor,
on a French music-hall, do you ever see the personages
of Balzac or Victor Hugo portrayed. Not that these
others were lesser artists. They were greater, and far
more conscious and scrupulous. This leads me back to
the fact that a work of art cannot exist in isolated purity,
the artist has to select and refine, and give back something that conveys a meaning. Even more true is this
of a tradition, which if it conveys nothing from one
period to another is misnamed.

Beneath Dickens and Thackeray, and never in the

first class, come Bulwer Lytton and Disraeli, romanticists who knew English life only from above, the now fashionable Trollope, who never knew it very deeply, and the more versatile Kingsley in whom the mere portraiture of manners is diversified by elements of pamphleteer and preacher, and, of all things, the adventure story. I think that *Hereward* and *Westward Ho!* are more this than traditional novels.

One of the marks of our subject is, however, the extent and degree of excellence to which women could engage in the calling. Ask yourselves how far women have influenced English poetry or drama since 1800, and compare the result with Jane Austen—and more lately with the Brontës and George Eliot, to name only those of real value to the tradition. The Brontës, more especially Charlotte, of course, give an imaginative rendering of English life which is in the direct succession. Humour and pathos, incident arising out of the clash of accurately seen and portrayed character, unlaboured satire with moral purpose are all there, but cast in a particular mould which could not be mistaken for masculine production. Even Professor Saintsbury refrains from defining the particular influence. I will only hazard the suggestion that there was suppressed yearning for female emancipation. I think this is less noticeable in George Eliot; I do not think that I could tell that her writing is not that of a man. It is variable, of course, and has certain specific defects, but I think that *Middlemarch*, for instance, is right in the centre of the tradition started by Richardson, strengthened by Fielding, and so heavily emphasized by Dickens. The question is not without importance in view of subsequent events. We have been discussing a tradition, passing through the difficult stages of early growth. We have seen it avoid the perversions that attacked and the weakness that debilitated the same form in other countries, or other literary forms in its own. You will see how rich and varied a tradition it had become when you hear about experiment in it. But as you may have observed in other forms of life, this very strength and immunity became in itself a danger. The technique of the novel is entirely mental. No paraphernalia are required save ink and paper. Even the typewriter is a twentieth-century complication. Thus, literally anybody can set up as a novelist, however soon he may relapse into the writer of one novel or merely of a rejected manuscript. This would not be worthy of attention had it not coincided with that extraordinary flush of prosperity, unique in the world, which marks the last third of the nineteenth century and has persisted in spite of the grave events of recent decades. This created an enormous demand for the novel, and called forth a correspondingly unheard-of supply. A further stimulus was imported by the English, rather than British, distrust of theory, and of academic manner. Thus the critical body is far less in charge of novel production and consumption than elsewhere, and those functions tend to continue on a commercial rather than an artistic basis. To define the tradition of the English novel now becomes very difficult. What tradition does the cataract of modern novels follow?

I think we can only say that in the main it is a weakly romantic one. The love interest and the happy ending have become so fastened upon this literary form as to crystallize, apparently permanently, upon its new mechanical dimensions, the cinema and the wireless.

English non-mordant and generally physical humour,
English proneness to be deeply affected by pathos—
and pathos is a perishable element—all tend to this
result. So does the English view of morals that makes
it almost obligatory that the hero should be good and
successful, brave and safe. The blame, if it can be
fixed at all, is largely Robert Louis Stevenson's. He
knew how to pack into his novels, that are equally
entitled to rank as boys' books, such a chain of breath-
less narrative, that he became the supreme entertainer.
Do not suppose I am carping at him. He lived his
adventures, died early, and had no truck with the happy
ending or love interest as such. But he had an immense
popularity, and although himself a legitimate descen-
dant of Defoe has had a thousand imitators who are not.

The trouble lies, I believe, in the fact that Stevenson
was so engrossed in living like Robinson Crusoe, with
tuberculosis always keying him up to the tension of risk,
that the weightier elements slipped out of his work.
Although he was profoundly concerned with style, his
outlook on life was necessarily uncritical, and when this
is imitated, as it is in enormous bulk, it makes the modern
quasi-adventure story. Even when the original scenery
is forgotten, and the venue is between the motor-car
and the manicure parlour, the same smooth superficiality
is detected, and that is why sometimes, when you look
at a railway bookstall, you feel as though you were gaz-
ing at a sea of treacle clogged with those little pink and
green sweets called 'hundreds and thousands'.

Amid such an ocean, what rocks can we discern that
show that the English novel still has a firm, bony
structure enclosing it and dictating its future, if any?

First of all we must recur to an accident that has

profound consequences to our survey. We are talking about the English novel. Now a very important phase of English life, the conscious, responsible Imperialism of the 'nineties, whose chief exponent is Mr. Kipling, is almost entirely expressed by him in grouped stories that are not our business.

At the furthest possible point of contrast, the one attempt at founding a definite literary school in England, by Arnold, Pater, and Wilde, yielded only two novels which have had little or no effect on the main tradition. Who then carried on the torch from the deaths of Dickens and Thackeray? It is very difficult to say. Three great figures dominated the latter half of the nineteenth century, and survived until yesterday—I speak of course of George Meredith, Henry James, and Thomas Hardy.

The first two we may take together. One English and the other American by birth, they wrote the prose comedy of manners in the Richardson limits, but with no other similarity to their forerunner. Meredith was touched with the romantic spirit, but the strong characteristic of both was an intense and complicated mental activity and a fluid sensibility, which enabled them to explore and record every slightest impression which the rather attenuated incidents of their stories caused in the brains of their characters. It may even be wondered if they did not both record more impressions than the average human being ever experienced. Their styles, widely differing, agree in being extremely involved, full of parentheses and inversions.

They certainly have few imitators, and I am not clear as to their effect on the tradition unless they helped to liquefy and expand mental processes. I should have been almost inclined to leave them to my colleague as experiments had it not been that the omission of two names of such weight and power, undoubted genius and great industry—James wrote forty books and Meredith two volumes of poetry besides many novels—required anyhow some explanation. Further, they both have another than a purely literary interest. James shows the English novel as common to two hemispheres, and indeed to all corners of the earth in which the tongue of our islands is spoken. Meredith excels perhaps in the delineation of female mentality and may stand, far more prominently than Charlotte Brontë or George Eliot, for the emancipation of the novel in the matter of sex. I am not sure that you could swear that some of his work—did you not know—had not been written by a woman. I feel sure he had an influence in the breaking down of the ancient ecclesiastical sex barrier.

Thomas Hardy stands quite alone: it is not for me really to point out how he has enriched the tradition. He was a great experimentalist, but I cannot leave him out. I have called the novel the Comedy of Manners written in prose. That is a weak description. The Comedy of Domesticity is nearer. In the novel we are not in realms supernal or infernal, as we are frequently with poetry. We are on the solid earth, not the actual, but simulated earth, so near to biography, history, and topography as to infringe sometimes the law of libel. To regard domestic incident as being just as thrilling as bloodthirsty escapades in remote lands, is one of the features of the novel. The spirit of Sir John Mandeville must occupy the body of Smith. It is the reverse of the saga process in which real people become legendary, for it involved making legendary, or rather typical people, real. Now in Hardy this reached the point of taking a definite piece of England, calling it Wessex, and thinly disguising geographical names. And yet, such was the cosmic point of view in Hardy, that he sees the earth, a tiny planet, revolving in infinite space, no greater than the flowers in a Dorsetshire lane. This had a twofold effect, for while, on the one hand, it drove out of his work all that warm, comfortable, personal sentiment that is so attractive in Dickens, it supplied an almost superhuman impersonality which is necessary, unless the strong didactic or moral influence, always present in English art, is to produce a very biased picture of life. I do not disguise from you that Hardy had his faults, and that he felt his relationship to the British public so acutely that it is said that he deliberately left the novel and took to poetry, which may or may not have suited his genius better. I leave the rest concerning him to my colleague.

Behold us then, arrived at the 'nineties, at a period from which the tradition is carried on by novelists who are still living and writing. This renders my task extremely difficult, but I must perforce say something of them, if only to state my belief, that, in spite of a keen anxiety as to some aspects of the novel in the twentieth century, and a feeling of great responsibility that you must share with me, there is a great comfort in the fact that we can say confidently that the best tradition is being maintained in a fashion that was never worthier.

Let us survey, for a moment, the general situation. A considerable part of the vitality of English literature lay outside the novel. Not only Mr. Kipling but figures as important as Mr. Shaw and Sir James Barrie preferred, with negligible exceptions, other forms.

Of the important, but not closely related group of writers who wrote the best novels, Joseph Conrad was a Pole of genius who used the methods of psychological analysis of motive and feeling, to as great a degree as, if in a different manner from, James and Meredith, upon the adventure story. It is not possible to gauge by his case the effect of the importance of the progress of literary tradition on the Continent, for Conrad was more than ordinarily susceptible to this. But Mr. Galsworthy and Mr. Bennett have, I think, both admitted to being influenced by the school of writing in France that follows Flaubert and de Maupassant, and one of them by the extreme sensitiveness displayed by the Russians Turgeniev and Tolstoi. This is as it should be, and shows that our tradition is by no means ossified and insular. If you add to the two I have named, Mr. Wells, who has, I think, derived less from foreign examples, you have living to-day three writers whom I do not hesitate to qualify, to their faces, as being of the very first rank within the limits of the tradition we have been following. I believe that I am just in claiming them as traditional novelists rather than as experimentalists. They are nearer to Dickens and Thackeray, Fielding and Jane Austen, than they are to James and Meredith and Hardy. The involved style, the intricate mentality, the rather cold impersonal view of very obvious local scenery seems to have run its course, and permitted a reversion closer to original type. Yet I do not feel sure that our living three have not benefited by the efforts of their immediate predecessors. After James and Meredith, it must have been easier to find in the psychological adventure of the human spirit an amply sufficient romance, without being obliged to recur to the physical incident of Defoe, Stevenson, or even Conrad. And after Hardy it must have been easier to maintain that impersonality that is one of the achievements of our great moderns, permitting them, as it does, to allow their characters to grow like living people instead of being jerked by wires like marionettes.

All else, in our great moderns, relates, I think, farther back. They all write that domestic comedy, as it was written before the weak romanticism became so widespread. The love interest with them falls into its proper place, and the happy ending occurs, or fails to occur, according to the laws of nature, as it does in the great dramatists of the medieval or classic schools. This again enables them to arrive at the imperative climax that signs and seals a work of art by inevitable instead of artificial stages.

Further, Messrs. Bennett and Galsworthy have other means than direct address to their readers, to convey their moral, social, in some cases, almost political propaganda. For they are not either of them that vapid thing, an artist for art's sake. They are human beings, treading our British earth and deeply concerned with its destinies. For this purpose they yoke their satire—which even in Dickens and Thackeray sometimes seems rather plastered on to the main structure, like ornament on an ill-proportioned building—to the aspiration towards perfection, so that it arises from the natural irony of existence. Both frequently employ the mere passage of time as a means of accumulating that modifying stream of incident that wears down the most solid-looking human structures and slowly and logically moves on the mortal drama. Both are writers of connected groups of novels, well known to you, which permit of this effect, for we all 'date' from some moment or incident when we were at our very best. Then life passes on, and in giving their turn to others, unconsciously relates us in our true value to the whole. Thus, it is sufficient to live, as the characters in their books live, to have a story. It is not the rather hopelessly inert philosophy of Hardy. You know the line of Amiel; 'Que vivre est difficile, O mon cœur fatigué!' Our English novelists have a vision saner and more robust. Mr. Wells stands slightly apart. The other two use the pamphlet on occasions that justify it, to express their views on current events. So does Mr. Wells, but there is more deliberately didactic purpose in his books, I think he will admit. This does not mean that he is farther from, but that he is nearer to, the eighteenth-century tradition. All three have produced a large body of first-class work.

Thus stands, so far as I can see, the tradition of the English novel. I have left the short story and all consideration of the effects of certain schools of criticism and cognate matters on one side, because it seems to me important to impress on you that this tradition does not rest on the shoulders of a few great writers, it rests upon you. I leave my subject with a nineteen-eighteen feeling. Do you remember the headline of a newspaper of that date? 'All is quiet on the Western Front, but the situation is not without danger. The morale of the troops is excellent'—Is it? You are the troops. If you buy and read, and allow to be bought and read without comment, stories that are shallow and silly, mechanical imitations, then the English novel will die, and no best seller in all his glory can save it. The tradition of which I have spoken is a national trust, like the National Gallery, or as the National Theatre would be, or Opera House if we had one (and we are the only civilized country in Europe that hasn't). But the tradition of the novel is not housed in concrete form in some well-guarded building. Its weakness is that it is embodied in a form of art that can be sold in packets like tea or cigarettes. It is always so easy to buy the worst, particularly in your London life where everything must be so glib and expedient from the morning train to the evening wireless. London has played a great, a unique part in English history, and the tradition of the novel is part of it. But it still rests with you individually to see that it does not sink to the place that Nineveh and Hollywood have played in their national history.

EXPERIMENT IN THE NOVEL

By J. D. BERESFORD

WHEN I began to consider the subject of this paper, I was instantly confronted by the difficulty of defining a recognizable tradition in English fiction to which I might conclusively point the exceptions. No doubt we all have some vague conception of what a novel is or should be, and we can be fairly sure as to the ingredients that it ought to contain. We feel that there should, for instance, be a love-story in most cases, some kind of plot, and a general movement towards complication followed by a denouement, whether in its derivative sense of a crisis or in its original sense of an unravelling or unknotting.

But if we were to take these simple essentials, shape them into a canon, and apply it to the masters of English fiction, we should find that nearly all of them had written one or more novels which did not comply with our rule. We might, for example, give good marks to *Jane Eyre* and hesitate over *Villette*, include *The Tale of Two Cities* and turn down *David Copperfield*. And we should seldom be rewarded by the complete sense of satisfaction experienced by the collector who marks down the indisputable type, in our attempt to file the works of Jane Austen, George Meredith, Thackeray, or Anthony Trollope.

The truth is that the type of novel confined by a neat and shapely plot, centring round an elaborated incident and developing a problem that it is the author's ambition to solve, convincingly and satisfyingly, is found most

often in the works of the minor writers. Our best
novelists have always been experimenters.

Nevertheless, since we must have some conception
of tradition in our minds, it may be as well to extend
our definition to cover, say, four recognizable orders of
fiction. The first is the neat, completed novel that
follows more or less the rule I have indicated. *Jane
Eyre* will do well enough for our type, and it is worthy of
remark that we should have had to descend below the
highest level of Charlotte Brontë's achievement in order
to find the nearest example to our requirements in this
form.

The second is some version of the life-story. We have
as a rule a central figure, man or woman, who need not
necessarily be too heroic, and we follow this protagonist
through a series of adventures, more or less protracted,
whether to success, failure, or death. *David Copperfield*
is a good illustration of this method, but it has such
variants as *Vanity Fair* in which the figure of Becky does
not appear in every scene. I might add *Pride and
Prejudice*, which if it treats but of one determining movement in the life of Elizabeth Bennet, falls appropriately
in this division. The writer's prime ambition in each
case was to portray the life of every day as he or she
observed it, handicapped only by the provision that it
was essential to tell a moving story.

The third division will include all historical and
romantic fiction, that is to say, stories of a period in
which the author is not living. This gives us a very
generous limit and we may cite the perfect type of
episodical romance in Stanley Weyman's *Under the Red
Robe*, and the general development of a broad historical
background for a large group of characters as in

Ivanhoe, or even such satirical fantasies as *Gulliver's Travels*. This is, in fact, the great romantic group and its edges may be left exceedingly vague.

Lastly, we have what is surely the original fount of all fiction, the adventure story, more or less of the type that is commonly defined in our days as the picaresque. The father of this school was Homer, who set so high a standard for it that we have never been able to do better. And so inclusive was the original type in this sort that in the *Odyssey* we even find a heroic love-story worked in at the end.

If, then, I may count these four styles as covering all the essentials of traditional fiction, we can begin by taking a glance here and there at certain instances of experiment, outside—though perhaps only just outside —these four groups, as essayed by the writers whose works may be regarded as 'classical', that is to say, approved by the judgement of posterity as being worthy of immortality.

To do this I propose first to take a very early English writer of fiction, born thirty years before that 'father of the English Novel', Samuel Richardson, who though he too was truly an experimenter in his own day—and did reasonably well out of his experiment—was one of the founders of the traditions it is my business to avoid. This writer is, of course, Daniel Defoe, whose method in certain works is as modern as the twentieth century.

In such books as *Moll Flanders*, he did nothing more than play on a variant of Homer's theme, substituting an immoral female heroine for the wily Odysseus. And even for this he had some precedent in the efforts of still earlier writers such as Thomas Deloney and Aphra Behn. *Robinson Crusoe*, also, written like most of his best work after he had reached the age of sixty, though truly an experiment in 1719, founded another of our recognizable traditions. But in the *Journal of the Plague Year*—or *The History of the Plague* as it was called in the second edition—Defoe made an experiment that still remains in the experimental class.

The essence of it lies in the telling of historical fact as fiction—not, as in the later historical novel, by the invention of imaginary characters and incidents to furnish the desiderated story of love and adventure as is Harrison Ainsworth's treatment of the same plague in *Old St. Paul's*, but to set life going again as it were, in a vanished setting: to give colour and animation to historical events by describing them in the manner of an eyewitness. In a sense this is nothing but a brighter kind of history, but the test of its fictional quality as applied by the novelist is in the search for invented conversations. If you find in any book a verbatim report of dialogue that imitates the manner of normal human speech, that book may be written down as a work of fiction.

The History of the Plague is done in the retrospective manner, the events recorded took place in Defoe's life-time although he was only six years old in 1665; and no doubt some at least of his material was taken from the accounts of eyewitnesses. But although a man may remember the purport of a certain conversation after forty years, no one will remember more than a stray phrase or two at most of the actual give and take of the original dialogue, and when we find it set down *in extenso* we may be quite sure that the author is drawing upon his powers of invention. Finally, if we be very expert in criticism we shall recognize the fact that no

novelist is able completely to conceal his own manner-
isms or tricks of style, even in the attempt to report the
speech of characters assumed to be on a level, of education or what not, entirely different from that of the
author himself. 'Which fiddle-strings is weakness to
expredge my nerves this night,' says Betsy Prig, and we
instantly recognize the method of Charles Dickens.
Finally, I must add here that without recourse to verbatim conversations, it is almost impossible for a novelist
to get an effect of naturalism in telling a story. Speech
is the clue to character, even when, as in the works of
George Meredith, the characters speak the master's
idiom.

Now if we are to draw any inferences from the fact
that Defoe's story of the Plague remains an experiment
while his *Robinson Crusoe* or Samuel Richardson's
Pamela have crystallized into a tradition, we must assign
a reason for the difference between the two types. It
is true that a few historical novels here and there approach the principles of Defoe's method. Such recent
examples as Maurice Hewlett's *Richard Yea-and-Nay* and
The Queen's Quair are rather readings of the characters
of Richard and Mary Queen of Scots, than endeavours
to tell an interesting fiction in a picturesque setting.
More recently still Morley Roberts has told the life of
George Gissing as a novel and Mr. Beckhofer Roberts the
life of Charles Dickens. But we can definitely say that
Defoe's example in this kind has been so little followed
that it cannot be counted a tradition.

The obvious reason for this is that the *Journal of the
Plague Year* does not hold the mind of the average
reader by the grip of a developing story. The assumed
narrator has no moving adventures, neither his personal

life nor his character is developed, and though the book survives and can still be read with living interest, it fails as a fiction because it moves to no crisis, and as history because its facts are not authenticated. For these reasons, presumably, the authors who succeeded Defoe were not inspired to copy it, and this successive copying is the sole means by which an experiment becomes in the course of the centuries an accepted tradition.

But I must note here one further deduction to which I shall return later, namely, that this book of Defoe's has a value for us as a precedent in experiment because it represents an essay in what I may call ultra-realism. For Defoe was a realist if ever there was one, and the various developments of the effort to get as near the truth of life as is possible for our limited intelligences will represent the more important aspect of those exceptions in fiction with which I propose to deal when I come to contemporary literature.

Before I do that, however, one further distinction is necessary. There are three kinds of experiment that can be made on the production of a piece of fiction. These are experiments in matter, method, and manner. There may, of course, be a combination of these in a single book, such as Wyndham Lewis's *Childermass*, but we need not bother ourselves with subdivisions.

The first class needs little definition. William Beckford's *Vathek* might serve as an instance or even James Morier's *Hajji Baba*; or any fiction of the kind that hovers between fairy tale and adventure in an eastern setting rather in the manner of *The Arabian Nights*. *Don Quixote* was an experiment in matter. Rudyard Kipling's *Kim*, Herman Melville's *Moby Dick*, Conrad's

Nigger of the Narcissus—these represent experiment for our purpose because such fictions are very difficult to classify in any of the four classes into which we divided the traditional types. They are, in short, books of the kind that surprise and no doubt frequently disappoint the library subscriber who settles down hopefully to be entertained by a 'nice story'.

The distinction between method and manner is a little more subtle and technical. By method I intend here only the means of approach to the writing of a novel; the means with which we are most familiar being that of the omniscient novelist who knows the hearts and minds of all his characters. All our famous novelists have employed it, Dickens, Thackeray, Hardy, Scott, Jane Austen. The next is that of the pretended auto-biography, the whole story being told in the first person. Beyond these there is the method of limiting the author's knowledge to the consciousness of a single character, through whose contacts with life alone can we have any knowledge of the other persons of the story; finally, such devices as telling our stories by means of letters—a device that dates back to Samuel Richardson—or of a diary.

If, then, we may count these means of approach as covering the tradition we must regard any more eccentric means of approach as an experiment, and although I do not propose to linger over this development, I should certainly include the method of telling a story at second hand as an experiment that has not succeeded to the point of claiming rank as a tradition.

In *Wuthering Heights* Emily Brontë tells the better part of her story through one of the characters, the relatively insignificant one of the housekeeper. Per-

sonally, that method does not please me, destroying my
sense of reality. There are certain conventions that we
must accept, such as that I referred to in the matter of
detailed conversations when the book purports to be
written out of the memory of one or more of the persons
concerned. But when we have an uneducated woman
using the language of Emily Brontë to describe the
scenes of that tragic history, I feel that the invention
becomes overstrained. It would not matter nearly so
much if we were allowed to forget the interposition of
this amazingly gifted woman, but we are reminded of
it at every interval in the recital. To me, that seems
a failure of artistry. It was no doubt easier for Emily
Brontë to use that method, but the easiest method is not
always the best.

Conrad, too, experimented freely with the second-hand
method of approach; but having assumed in Marlowe
a raconteur of genius, we are less disturbed in *Lord Jim*,
for example, when we are reminded of his mediumship
now and again. Marlowe is, in effect, Conrad, and
though the experienced reader knows very well that
no man ever spoke as Conrad wrote, the convention
does not upset too disturbingly our feeling for realism.
In *Chance*, however, the method was subjected to a still
more severe strain and the recital removed to third and
even fourth hand, the report of a report of a report, all
of them in the original idiom. That, indeed, was an
experiment in method that was not worth repeating;
though it served its purpose so well on this occasion that
this was the first of Conrad's books that achieved anything approaching to a popular success. I must add,
however, that the success was not due to the eccentricity
of the method.

Our third class of exception falls under the head of 'manner', and as that may in most cases be written 'literary style', we shall find a little difficulty in making out the exact degree of eccentricity that might differentiate the exception from the tradition. There may be an unbridgeable difference between the manner of William Surtees in *Jorrocks* and that of Hardy in *The Return of the Native*, but we recognize both as being in the sound tradition of story-telling. But we may, perhaps, hesitate over the works of Meredith and Henry James. What differentiates them is the tendency to obscurity. Our English tradition in this sort is all for direct narrative, and when authors such as these seek for the finer shades of expression to the interruption of the story, we may, perhaps, be inclined to include them among the exceptions. And Meredith, at least, has found no imitators for the excellent reason that it is not in his case the idiosyncrasy of style that we might wish to copy but the erudition and intelligence that lie behind it. I recently re-read *The Adventures of Harry Richmond* and was inclined to deplore the loss of a great story-teller in Meredith, for he tended continually to obscure rather than to clarify his narrative powers in his later books.

Now if we apply our threefold test to the novels of those accepted writers from Defoe onwards whose works have been acclaimed by the critics as worthy to survive, we shall find very few that have not already been indicated in the application of the test in question. Most notable among them, perhaps, is *Tristram Shandy*, for I can think of no other novel—I suppose we may call it a novel?—in which the hero is not conclusively born until the last chapter. But Laurence Sterne was certainly not in the tradition, and it is doubtful if we can

properly refer to his *Sentimental Journey* as a fiction.
Beyond that Swift's *Tale of a Tub*, though it may find
a classification under satires, has enough of the imaginative story-telling quality to deserve mention here. But
these examples, I think, include all the first-class literature that comes within the limit of this survey. Below
that level we should have for the most part only
'freakish' books to record, such as Mary Shelley's
Frankenstein or various experiments by Bulwer Lytton,
works for which we demand some kind of No Man's
Land, a division that will include the dead and the
dying, though here and there may be found a body or
two with life enough to carry on if we care to attempt
the effort of rescue—a work, I may note, for which
there is always a sufficiency of volunteers.

Now looking back over this very brief historical
sketch of the experiments in fiction made by well-known
writers who are no longer living, we may glance at one
or two useful deductions. The first has already been
touched upon, and is that the experimental in this kind
remains experimental only so long as it is not copied by
succeeding writers. Henry Fielding was an experimenter, and his first novel, *The History of the Adventures
of Joseph Andrews and of his friend Mr. Abraham Adams*,
was begun as a burlesque of Richardson's *Pamela*. But
just as in the case of Dostoievsky, who began *The
Possessed* solely in order to pillory the figure of his
contemporary Turgeniev, Fielding's genius was too
strong for him and the satire faded out under the
influence of the fascination of his own story. But neither
Fielding nor Richardson, nor for the matter of that any
one of half-a-dozen experimenters in the same sense,
can come under our title, because their experiment

was the founding of a tradition. From this it follows that in any historical examination of our examples, we have been driven to examine only the experiments that failed in the sense that they found no successors to copy them, either because the example did not appear to be a profitable one to follow, or because, as in the case of George Meredith, it was too difficult to imitate.

Nevertheless, among these apparent failures we may find the first suggestions, however tentative, that lay behind the many daring and possibly formative experiments that have marked the fiction of the last thirty years. The first of these is that experiment of Defoe's upon which I lingered. For I find there the germ of the movement towards an ever-increasing naturalism that has now reached, and I believe passed, its climax. Defoe, as I have said, was a great realist, and although such a book as his *History of the Plague* found no imitators among successful novelists in the succeeding generations, when a little before the turn of the century there was a noticeable reaction against a rather romantic, sentimental period, it was the realist method that began to be so earnestly worked. And with such startling results.

The second instance of an old suggestion blooming into new and almost unrecognizable forms is to be found in Swift's *Tale of a Tub* and *Gulliver's Travels*; for in these books we may trace the first tendency to incorporate broad political and social satire—as opposed to the more personal satire of manners—in the form of imaginative fiction. And because this is the less important of the two developments I propose to follow, I shall treat it first, and take as my chief exponent the works of H. G. Wells.

Mr. Wells has, of course, been from the very beginning frankly an experimenter. Even at the outset of his career, when he consciously attempted to follow the conventions of story-telling laid down by tradition, he found the limitations too restricting for his genius. But we need not linger over any inquiry into his earlier resistances which are of the type familiar to us in the work of many first-class novelists. What I propose to examine here is Wells's development of the sociological essay in a form that is recognizably that of fiction. Charles Kingsley certainly did something of the same kind in *Yeast* and *Alton Locke*, but I can remember no other precedent in the work of the Victorian novelists; and the most original critic would hardly dare to say that Wells derived from Charles Kingsley.

We find the beginnings of this method in *Tono-Bungay*. Here it is less marked by reason of the fact that the book is written in the first person, and George Ponderevo as the autobiographer is at liberty to hold up his story in order to comment on the condition of a society that would allow such a little swindler as his uncle to draw an immense fortune out of the pockets of the credulous investor, or of the still more credulous believer in patent medicines. But thereafter, the socio-logical essay begins steadily to invade, in some case almost to exclude, the human narrative. In *The New Machiavelli*, although it again has the excuse of being written in the first person, we find the analysis of the political situation intruding to the complete occultation of the story as such; and the only concessions made to the habitual novel-reader in the course of these extended samples of sociological tract are occasional incidents thrown in to revive his attention. While in such a recent book as *William Clissold*, the story has ceased to be the *raison d'être* of the work, and crops up only at uncertain intervals.

Here, then, we have an author who under the cloak of fiction—a cloak sometimes very carelessly adjusted and flying open with every impatient stride taken by the wearer—has set out his personal opinions on every aspect of the broad sociological problems of our own day. In *The New Machiavelli* we have an essay in criticism on the methods and restrictions of modern politics, particularly restrictions, for Mr. Wells is all for freedom of every possible kind. *The Undying Fire* is a treatise in the form of dialogue on a phase of religious thought. *The Research Magnificent* is an analysis of fundamental social problems. And these expressions of Wells's social and religious idealisms are not conveyed in the manner of such political novels as Disraeli's *Coningsby*, *Sybil*, and *Tancred*, but are stated, in some cases without any disguise whatever, as the author's own opinions. In imagination we may picture him, suddenly harassed by that cloak of fiction, snatching it off and hurling it across the room, in order that he may give free play to the passion of his conviction that nothing but our inertia, our blindness, our stultifying adherence to a foolish rule of thumb, stands between us and a beautiful world of order and liberty. As he writes he is so sure that Utopia is but just round the corner if only we would take the few necessary steps to reach it. Afterwards, we may assume, that mood is followed by a reaction. We may have a glimpse of him entering his study in a reflective, morning mood, absent-mindedly picking up and adjusting the discarded cloak before he sits down to write. He takes a glance or two here and there, no doubt, at the outpourings of yesterday, folds his cloak a shade closer about him, and begins resolutely: 'And now I come to the most evasive and difficult part of my story, which is to tell how Isabel and I . . .'

But this mechanical mixture of fiction and sociological essay is not the only form in which he has experimented. Before he began his reform propaganda, he was a romancer of the same order as Jules Verne, and gave us various scientific romances that my boys to-day find as fascinating as did their father before them. Yet even in this, his most imaginative mode, in which it would seem that the story must be the prime essential, Mr. Wells's imagination already begins to play about his mission to humanity. In the first of the romances, which was also the first of his books, other than a collection of occasional papers and sketches, we can see the leanings towards what was at that time (1895) a more or less orthodox State Socialism. When the inventor of the Time Machine takes his flight into the future he finds social conditions that are presumed as the outcome of the class-war. As a social prediction it would, of course, be dismissed by the Wells of only a few years later, but even in that first of his books, we find the narrative stammering now and again as a consequence of the author's political (they were political, then) convictions. The same theme is a trifle more explicit in *The Wonderful Visit*, published the same year, but fades out almost completely in *The Island of Dr. Moreau* and *The War of the Worlds*. But in *When the Sleeper Wakes* we have another prophecy of the outcome of the class-war, and there the story again suffers in the cause of sociology. Later with one interlude, *The Sea Lady*, the sociological theme, expanding steadily beyond the restrictions of politics, gradually gets the upper hand even in the Wellsian romances. It is well to the fore already with *In the Days of the Comet*; it flashes into a fierce criticism of the futility of war in *The War in the Air*, finally takes hold and pushes the story into the background in *The World Set Free* (1914), and is continually present in our minds in such later romances as *Men Like Gods* and *The Dream*.

The third form in which Mr. Wells has mixed the essay and fiction forms is to reverse the process. In *A Modern Utopia* we understand from the outset that the essay on the reconstruction of society in the ideal state is the essential theme of the book, but it is rendered a little more palatable to the average reader than, say, the straight essay method of *New Worlds for Old*, by occasional reversions to the form of a fiction. That, however, was a method that was dropped after a single experiment. We may find a parallel for it in William Morris's *News from Nowhere*.

Now, before I go on to glance at the work of one or two other experimenters in the same field, and consider the tendency and possible development of fiction mixed with explicit propaganda, I want to pause for a minute or two over the reason for Mr. Wells's experiments. It has always been the fashion among the critics to find fault with the Wellsian method. It is, indeed, a temptingly easy thing to do. If we begin with any sort of canon deduced from the study of the works of our greatest novelists, we see at once that Wells's fiction cannot be ranged either with that of his predecessors or with that of his more conventional contemporaries such as Galsworthy and Bennett. We can accuse him quite justly under cover of our secure critical canons of lack of form, of lamentable failures in construction and artistry generally. He is the great Nonconformist in this kind, and outside the pale of our orthodoxy. Middleton Murry, one of our ablest critics, has said that Wells is never an artist except in his short stories.

But while I admit that that is true from one point of view, Wells is, nevertheless, one of our great English men of genius, and I want you to remember that all the canons whether in prose or verse had their origin in the work of men of genius. And if we are to assume that all the best forms have already been discovered, that any further violation of the literary rules we have been able to deduce from our study of the great writers—many of whom began by being iconoclasts, breakers of the sacred image—is to be condemned because it is outside the traditions; then we must be content to admit, also, that our literature has ceased to grow, and that which has ceased to grow is a dead thing.

Wherefore having found a reason for H. G. Wells, and made apology to those critics who oppose all rites not specified in their own rubric, let us consider him as innovator and inquire whether there is any probability of this method being adopted by future generations.

In the first place he is beyond all question a brilliant novelist. Neither Galsworthy nor Bennett has the same power of conveying an intense effect of reality. Nevertheless he is not among the great creators of character, partly perhaps because his vivid realism influences him to portray the familiar man and woman of every day rather than the rarer, more pronounced type. But whether he is picturing man in face of a world revulsion or Kipps rolling huckaback, his characters seem to come straight out of life rather than out of the imagination of the novelist. In this particular, he borrows from nature rather than teaches us to observe her in her more eccentric moods.

But greatly as I am tempted to enlarge upon this, to me, peculiarly fascinating theme, it does not fall within the scope of this lecture, and I must hurry on to display the picture of our brilliant novelist writing novels that the unfortunately low average represented by the library subscriber refuses to read. Briefly I find the reason in a fertility of idea equal to that of the great Frenchman Victor Hugo. But whereas Victor Hugo did, for the most past at least, keep his ideas apart, with Wells they are so closely related to one central idea, the reform of the world at large, that he cannot confine himself within the limits of any accepted form in his fierce urgency to expression. Wells the reformer, Wells the novelist, and Wells the journalist form an indivisible trinity; and as his mind is not divided into water-tight compartments when he sits down to write, the great flood of his genius cannot be confined by any set channel. We cannot liken the flow to anything but an inundation.

And for this reason we have good cause for believing that his example will find few imitators. He has not given us a new form, he has only displayed his contempt for all conventional limitations. And to imitate him successfully in that, the imitator must have an equal measure of genius.

Nevertheless, one other twentieth-century novelist has given us a couple of essays in this same mixture of fiction and criticism—criticism that is to say of our present social conditions. This novelist is Mr. Oliver Onions, who has never had the recognition he deserves.

In *Little Devil Doubt*, his criticism of the methods of modern journalism swamped his story, but in *Good Boy Seldom* he gave us what may be truly described as a model in this kind. There are two ostensible objects of attack: company-promoting in the manner of Ponderevo in *Tono-Bungay* and modern advertising. But at the back of both attacks lies the more subtle criticism of the exploitation of the industrious middle-class worker brought up on the principles of virtue inculcated by the famous Samuel Smiles. The book is written in the form of a biography of that Good Boy Seldom, James Enderby Wace; but there are passages in which the author presents his case directly to the reader while his characters are temporarily off-stage. The book is far more strictly confined within the novel form than the looser of Wells's books in this kind, but it is of the same order. Personally, I rank it very high among the productions of the Georgian novelists. Another experiment made by Mr. Onions, though of a very different kind, is to be found in the trilogy begun with *In Accordance with the Evidence*, continued in *The Debit Account*, and concluded by *The Story of Louie*. I am surprised that that experiment has not already found imitators. The reason is probably that none of our younger authors have had the talents, or the ambition, to attempt it.

Gilbert Cannan also may be ranked among recent authors who have more or less successfully combined the novel and the essay; but he lacked the steady purpose and the unifying idea that give a *raison d'être* to the Wellsian books and to *Good Boy Seldom*.

I hesitate, however, to put another author, this time unquestionably a man of genius, in the same class, although he, too, has a habit of breaking bounds and

fiercely addressing the reader in his own person. D. H.
Lawrence is truly an experimenter within our definition,
but not a propagandist in the same sense as Wells,
Onions (in the two books instanced), or even Gilbert
Cannan. We know very well in reading a book of
Lawrence's that the narrative may 'go to pot' at any
moment while he sets forth with that strange mixture
of eloquence and virulence peculiar to him, his analyses
and dissections of sex, but we feel that he is feverishly
seeking truth and self-conviction rather than attempting
to convert us to his own ideas. Our point is, however,
that he is not primarily a teller of stories. In such books
as *Sons and Lovers*, it is true we can read for the story
only, taking the divagations as little more than a legitimate embroidery of the background. But in *The Rainbow*
and in some later books the embroidered background
becomes of greater importance than the central figures
of the tapestry.

With this instance I propose to close my review of this
aspect of recent experiment in fiction. But before going
on to those developments of realism I foreshadowed,
I want to consider the possible effect that the marked
departure from tradition dared by our last group may
possibly have upon the future of the novel.

We must distinguish in the first instance between this
new platform for opinion and that provided under cover
of tradition by our old friend the 'novel with a purpose'.
In that form the moral, or even it may be the political,
lesson was brought home by writing a story to illustrate
it and sticking to the story. Dickens would take up
some contemporary scandal such as the practices of
certain Yorkshire schools or the horrors contingent
upon imprisonment for debt and put one or more of

his characters through the mill, so that we might witness their agonies. And I remember only one instance in which his moral indignation takes a form that holds up the narrative and has manifestly nothing to do with the movement of the plot. This instance is in *Nicholas Nickleby*, and it is Nicholas himself who is given a long speech for the purpose of exhibiting the wickedness of the contemporary theatre manager, a speech that is not even in character.

But between inventing a story to illustrate a social evil and using the novel as a vehicle for airing our opinions, venting our grievances, or attempting a political reformation, there is a very great difference. The novel as we know it, from its inception until the end of the nineteenth century, does set out to keep its story going and we expect the detail to be strictly relevant to that purpose. Such detail may be dull. There may be too much description of scenery, or of social conditions, as in *Alton Locke*, or an excess of religious argument, as in *Robert Elsmere*. A few people may become impatient of the dissertations on the natural history of whales and the methods of whalers in *Moby Dick*. But what we do not find in any of these classical examples is a sudden lowering of the curtain and a waiting stage while the author comes in front in order to tell us not only what he is up to with the figures of his drama but also, perhaps, what his opinions are on this and that.

Is there, then, any future for this compound of novel and essay? It will not, I admit, ever become popular with the Boots subscriber I have postulated as one of our reagents. But I do not see why there should not be a public for the mixture, if it is sufficiently well made.

It does obviously solve a problem for a certain kind of author, the kind who has a very great deal to say and has a natural inclination to say some of it in the form of fiction. If Wells had had to set out all he was burning to tell us in the strict narrative form, using his characters and inventing his incidents to illustrate his theme, but employing no other means, he would have had to write twice as many books as he has already produced, a present total of well over fifty volumes. Moreover, in this era of free verse why should we not accord equal liberty from the bonds of form to the writer of fiction? If a man has something to say and chooses to say it in his own manner, shall we condemn him because we subscribe to some convention or another, or because a certain class of novel-reader protests that she does like a story to be a story? Such a vehicle as this may never rise to the dignity of an art-form, but what proportion of modern fiction could be appraised as good art? One-tenth of one per cent.?

Let us come now to that development of ultra-realism. The tradition of the English novel has always been realistic in the main, and by realistic I intend the mode that inclines to portray the real rather than the ideal, that takes its body from life rather than from imagination. (Among first-class writers we have had but one pre-eminently romantic novelist, Sir Walter Scott.) But towards the end of the last century George Moore began what was then in effect an experiment in English realism. In *Esther Waters* he cast off the shackles of plot; his obvious purpose being to make his story real as well as his characters and setting.

Now this marks an important turning-point. George Moore was undoubtedly under the influence of the

French realists of the Flaubert School, as was also, though perhaps less obviously, his successor in this vein, Arnold Bennett. And the great declaration they made was for liberty. *Pamela, David Copperfield, The Newcomes* had indicated the line of this development, but had just kept within the limitation imposed by the necessity for telling a more or less conventional story. Moore, then Bennett, and after them a host of imitators claimed that any piece of life honestly and truly reproduced was a subject for fiction, no matter whether or not the piece selected for display showed any development in the course of the story. In what I count as the greatest achievement in this kind, Bennett's *Old Wives' Tale*, the story of two sisters is told from girlhood to death. One of them had interesting experiences, even suffered in the siege of Paris; the other spent a serenely uneventful life in the Five Towns. But throughout there is no movement towards any vital complication or crisis—such as the determining movement in David Copper-field towards his second marriage which constitutes the main 'plot' of that book—and at the end Constance and Sophia Baines die, exemplars of no virtue other than the slightly dour steadfastness of the Staffordshire character.

Now the next extension of the principle implicit in this claim is to eliminate the more marked incidents of human life, just those incidents, such as love and marriage, that have always been the favourite subject for fiction. Let us call those outstanding and inferenti-ally more interesting episodes the 'high spots', and come to the consideration of novels that seek to tell a story without reference to these sporadic crises in our history. Virginia Wolff's *The Voyage Out* may be taken as an early example, but the theory has been developed in what I may perhaps describe as its utmost purity by Miss Dorothy Richardson.

She is one of those inspired and yet deliberate experimenters who have founded a School. So able and famous a writer as Miss May Sinclair openly avowed discipleship in her novel, *Mary Olivier*. And the fact that that School has not flourished is probably due to the strong current that ever since the end of the War has been setting back so strongly in the direction of romance.

Miss Richardson sat down to write the story of her own life, in the person of Miriam Henderson, with the clearest possible conception of what she intended to do. She claimed, for example, that what I have referred to as the 'high spots' (a definition I have borrowed from her own conversation) were only so by reason of the emphasis that have been laid upon them by the novelists; and that in the adventure of the personality, which should be the true subject for the novelist, the 'high spots' are of an entirely different order. To demonstrate this contention Miss Richardson invented a new method. Many other novelists before her had told their stories through the consciousness of one of their characters, but Miss Richardson's liaison with the consciousness of Miriam Henderson is so close that we see nothing, hear nothing, feel nothing except through Miriam's senses.

Now as a logical consequence of this—and Miss Richardson is essentially logical in the development of her method—there must be a different record of movement in space and time. The consciousness is not always attentive to its present circumstances. While

I read this lecture to you, although sufficient of my attention is being devoted to the subject to ensure a reasonable effect of coherence, my thought may take a leap in space and time and I may for an instant or two be aware of myself in completely different surroundings and in another period of my life. To achieve that effect in a novel Miss Richardson had to invent a new method, and one of her aids to that end was the omission of the copula, whether a word, an explanatory sentence, or a movement in her story. In the series of books—nine of them have now been published—dealing with the experiences of Miriam Henderson, the personality of Miss Richardson, the writer, is entirely absorbed into that of Miss Richardson the experiencer. She cannot, therefore, come out and join up her account of incidents or emotions as all other novelists do by a few words or lines of condensed explanation; for to do that would be momentarily to forsake the consciousness of Miriam Henderson. Thus whereas the orthodox novelist would explain that his heroine left the house, went out by the garden gate, walked across two or three fields and entered the wood; Miss Richardson either skips all account of the transition, or if some emotion experienced in the transit be necessary to her unfolding of Miriam, we suffer it subjectively. We begin, for example, in the house, then suffer some reaction at the sight of a field of daffodils, and thereafter without further copula find ourselves responding to the influences of the Spring wood.

This is certainly the most daring and far-reaching experiment that has up to this point engaged our attention. We may find some precedent for it in the work of Marcel Proust, and I shall presently come to another just recognizably similar experiment in James Joyce's *Ulysses*. But Miss Richardson's work is, nevertheless, unique in fiction (none of her disciples has ever dared the full implications of her theory) and has a metaphysical value that is absent in Proust or Joyce.

For neither of these writers is inspired by the mystical quality that is peculiar to Miss Richardson. Joyce and Proust are objective in their methods more often than not. We are constantly aware of the person of the recorder as opposed to that of the experiencer. Dorothy Richardson has assumed the existence of a soul to which the consciousness has much the same relation that the intelligence has to the consciousness. In *Pointed Roofs*— the first of the Miriam Henderson series—and in all the subsequent volumes, the ebb and flow of Miriam's consciousness, touched now and again to vivid response, at other times somewhat drearily aware of the limitations of physical experience, is the sole agent of the author's expression.

As a consequence the 'high spots' of our earlier illustration differ completely in kind from those deemed most interesting for a physical record. The great moments of Miriam's experience are not found in moving adventure nor in moments of physical stress, but at those times when she is most keenly aware of herself in relation to the spirit that moves beneath and animates every phenomenon of the great phantasmagoria we know as life and matter. I am willing to maintain that the realistic method can go no farther than this, for reality is not a term that we can define, and the view of it differs with every individual. If, therefore, we wish to present an aspect of reality, we can do it consistently

only by assuming its presentation through the consciousness of a single individual.

Mr. Joyce's remarkable experiment, *Ulysses*, though
often referred to in connexion with the work of Dorothy
Richardson, is of another kind. He has taken one day
in the life of a Dublin bank clerk of Jewish origin, and
followed his experiences through that day. In this
account nothing that can be recorded has been omitted,
and among the experiences and necessities of human
life which it is possible to describe, many here appear
for the first time in literature. The literary manner of
this book is, also, unprecedented; since it is not written
in one manner but in many. Now and again we may
assume that Mr. Joyce is writing as it is most natural
for him to write, something as he wrote in his earlier
work, *Portrait of the Artist as a Young Man*. But the greater
part of this immensely long work is done in imitation
of the methods and styles of earlier writers, beginning
with an archaic form.

I do not propose to criticize Mr. Joyce's *Ulysses* in
this place. You will find all that is necessary under that
head in a long essay entitled *The Strange Necessity*, by
Miss Rebecca West. But I feel quite safe in saying that
this, perhaps the most eccentric experiment in the English
language, is not likely to be imitated. This not because
there are places described in *Ulysses* to which the ordinary
writer cannot follow Mr. Joyce, unless his novel is to
be published by subscription, beyond the range of a
police prosecution; but because it is doubtful whether
the attempt to set down every action, word, or thought
of one day in a life is worth doing. It is true that having
read *Ulysses* we know all that we could ever want to
know of the character of Leopold Bloom. But if our

ultra-realism, as I have called it, is to lead us only to the intensive study of such a subject as this, we should soon find ourselves in the attitude of the fakir who acquires holiness by seven years' unwavering contemplation of his own navel.

Looking back, I feel that I have taken you over some very strange ground in our brief survey of English realism from Daniel Defoe to James Joyce. On the way I have completely passed over some very famous names, most noticeably perhaps that of Thomas Hardy. But I have done this deliberately. Hardy, for instance, may be counted an experimenter of the same order as Meredith and Henry James. But his experimentalism, like theirs, was only in the expression of his own peculiar genius, and he played no tricks with the accepted form of the novel. His conception of life was individual and unquestionably exceptional, but his method and construction were as conventional as those of George Eliot; while his matter was that same stuff of life used by Dickens, Thackeray, or Trollope, seen through the particular pair of spectacles that were Hardy's only approach to reality.

I have already touched upon this metaphysical aspect of the novelist's relation to his material in speaking of the works of Dorothy Richardson, and now, in conclusion, I want to suggest to you that this great diversity of realities lies at the very heart of our subject.

I have in this lecture dealt exclusively with realist fiction. The romantics seldom, and the classicists never, enter the ranks of the experimenters. If I sit down to tell you a story out of my head, I shall choose inevitably an accepted, traditional form for the telling of it. By

E

that means my task will be made easier and you will more quickly understand. That road has been well laid and hedged, and why should we not follow it? But if I want to give you a nearer and nearer transcript of life as I have seen it, I find that it cannot be done by following the old signposts. And the more ardent the realism, the greater the necessity to experiment with new methods—until, as I think you will agree, a few modern writers have cast aside the last restrictions of classical form.

And with that gesture of liberation has gone also certain other restrictions, most prominently that of morals. Throughout the greater part of the nineteenth century, authors of genius such as Dickens and Thackeray would commit any fault of artistry rather than convey the impression that they were ready to condone an immoral action. A Sydney Carton or a George Wrayburne may atone for their careless living and find either heroic death on the scaffold or reward for their newly found virtue. But Becky Sharp must not prosper in her later days; poor harmless, trusting Little Em'ly must suffer to the uttermost; and a Steerforth be punished with death. It was the convention of the period and your successful novelist was afraid to tamper with it. Even Hardy suffered from a morbid morality in this connexion. But in the twentieth century our experimenters threw that convention overboard with a lot of other hamper. They meant to portray life as they saw it rather than as the moralists insist that it ought to be. And these two declarations of liberty, one for freedom of form and the other for freedom of material, lie behind all the experiments of recent fiction.

And, to get back to my metaphysical thesis, the

diverse shapes these experiments have taken are due to the fact that we all have different conceptions of reality. This has always been true, of course. No two people can ever see the same rainbow, and no two people have precisely the same impression of life. But in such an age as the Victorian, there is a greater tendency to merge the individual concept in the group. Dickens spoke the thought of the multitude. His success was due to the portrayal of types that the multitude could recognize. His thought was always a step or two ahead of that of the crowd he addressed, but the advance was always in the direction that the crowd was ready to take.

With the turn of the century and still more markedly as a result of the effects of the Great War, this group thinking has been broken up. There has been a manifest tendency in life and letters to pull down the old images. Society, government, religion are regarded as relatively unstable. There is an increasing body of people who are losing their faith in the old Institutions. And this scepticism has inevitably had its effect upon the novel. In the stable days of Queen Victoria, a Dickens, a Thackeray, or a Trollope could sit down to his desk with a comfortable sense of assurance that he knew the public for which he was writing and was himself a member of it. He might be an exceptional member, he might have gifts of eloquence, of observation, of insight, that raised him to a platform above the shoulders of the crowd he was addressing. But in the main their beliefs were his also, their reality and his own held enough points of likeness to permit freedom of communication. Also for public purposes, at least, there was but one morality.

E 2

Now that comfortable sense of assurance no longer exists for us, and the sincere novelist who writes because he, or she, wishes to express a personal relation to experience, must write as an individual and not as a member of a group. There is no longer the least assurance that the novelist's reality is the same as that of a sufficiently large body of people to ensure popularity.

And for this reason the line of demarcation between the realist and the story-teller who tends to fall into the romantic, traditional class has become much easier to draw when we deal with the present century. Indeed, we might almost say that we can find a test in the very tendency to experiment that is the proper subject of this lecture. Let me warn you, nevertheless, that it is a test that must be applied with great discretion, and bearing in mind the highly distasteful fact that in these days the practice of writing novels has become a trade rather than a calling. There is, for example, an easily distinguishable group, a very large one, no member of which will I consent to name, that writes with a finger on the public pulse. To be highly successful as a novelist in these days, it is essential to keep your audience in view while you are writing. But no great literature comes into the world by that road. When, as in the days of Dickens, the author was a member of his own public, he could give the best or very nearly the best that was in him without obscuring his genius. When he has deliberately to check his natural impulse to expression by the consideration of his public's disapproval, the result may evidence great craft but it can never be great Art.

So, in conclusion, I want you to regard the experimenters in fiction as those most worthy of your interest.

They are the pioneers who may found a tradition, although that tradition in its turn may presently be supplanted. If literature is to be a vital force, we must give it room to grow. And I will end as I began by reminding you that nearly all our great novelists have begun by being experimenters.

TRADITION IN POETRY

By EDMUND BLUNDEN

I AM, it appears, under the necessity of appearing in this tournament as an ancient and more or less venerable figure; others may come in aeroplanes, but I arrive on a bone-shaker; others may give a demonstration with electric stoves, but I freeze over my doleful brazier. Side-whiskers should have been worn. For tradition, in the eyes of many talented moderns, is what the comedian called 'so most antimacassar'. She is the mother of the antiquarians, the goddess of the belated, the spirit of the Sunday parlour where Martin Tupper's illuminated poems slumber with the padded photograph album on grey lace mats. It is this beldame who prevents the boys from using the grandfather clock as an air-gun target and the girls from staying out after, say, two in the morning. She has most brutally refused to have the picture of the old rustic bridge by the mill taken down, and Signor Triangulo Martini's study of a modern beer-bottle put up in its place. She is always singing her muddled versions of *Plantation Songs*, but when her innocent daughter attempted to bring in a selection called 'Le Chanteur de Jazz' she locked the piano. Willie came back from the University with a poem beginning:

> GRONK?
> What?
> Yes—
> I *said*
> GRONK;

everybody thought it original, but she sniffed, and remarked, 'I think you might moderate your language'.

Something like this, I am afraid, is the sketch of tradition which passes in some of the advanced circles. Others come perhaps to bury her, and I to praise her; but let us be quite certain of the identity of the deceased. Even her worst enemies allow her considerable merits, when it comes to the business of life. Those ladies and gentlemen who vociferate the necessity for beginning the arts all over again, for making the world's library and art gallery a desert and then indulging in a new creation, do not seek out the desert for their nearest suitable conditions of work. They are not wholly superior to tradition. When they think the coast is clear, they make love to her. They like the houses she has made, the gardens, the villages. They preach their gospel where she has during the course of many centuries prepared the right sort of tabernacles—her great national systems of civilization, for example, and her magnificently equipped cities, Paris, London, New York, Berlin, Vienna. It is only by virtue of tradition that the new style of a poet or sculptor has a chance, and is eagerly scrutinized—not so eagerly, of course, as an ideal commonwealth would ensure, but still, not too coldly in this disangelled existence. If we can suppose ourselves for a moment back in the pre-Roman Britain, we shall not easily find a cultural curiosity such as would require and support *The Times Literary Supplement*, let alone Mr. Eliot's poems. By a long and gradual education man has arrived at that state where it seems second nature to be acquainted with literature, music, philosophy, criticism, and art at large; where experiment is not hopeless, because tradition is after all prepared to look at it, and to reject or modify or even to entertain it in the course of some years.

Experiment itself seems obliged to seek materials and implements from the stores of tradition. Considering poetry and the poet as our subject, we must ask ourselves what can be expressed, in what way, and to whom. The poet attempts the description, criticism, and fulfilment of life; or, since definition here is always sure to be argued over, we may say that he has emotional disturbances which require to be ordered into a calmness of achievement; or, being vigorous, he sings out of sheer glory, and being weary, he sings for luck and comfort. If these guesses at his secret may pass, we are to presume that the verse he writes will be rhythmical and musical (rhythm and tune being capable of endless variety), and united from first to last in a harmony or design of metre, not breaking away as though from the back of a wagon an irregular fall of sacks of coal was going on. Verse, without further epithets, requires the sanction of natural movement; humanity cannot keep step with the noises of an accidental explosion in an ammunition dump. Ordered experience, recognizable rhythm—and, in addition to these, there is the melancholy fact that a poet must use known language. We may be sure that there is some sort of poetry in the communication of fishes, or the trumpeting of elephants, but we are incapable of borrowing those idioms, however aptly they might suit our unique emotions. A poet must employ the words and phrases that satisfy the mind and suit the throat of his fellow men.

In these three momentous problems incurred in the making of verse, tradition silently and powerfully intervenes. The poet is a noble creature, an epoch-making being, but behind him there is this mighty mother, and he is her poem. She brought him up, and in his impressible years gave him association, circumstance, sympathy, distaste, imagery, character—and probably bad handwriting. How much even of our emotions is our own? How much that stirs us is not due to the race, or family, or circle which sent us forward into the world? I cannot imagine that my own disposition is uncommon; I know from the evidence of my manuscripts that it is a poetical disposition, and an eager though not a fierce one; yet the things that have moved me, and the judgements I have formed, must be seen to originate in the type of life and feeling which I most fully experienced. Tradition, when in the person of my old schoolmaster she chose to train me on the English plan, to insist on my learning closely the Old Testament, songs of 'Cherry-Ripe' and 'I know a bank whereon the wild thyme blows', and maxims such as 'Trifles even lead to heaven' and 'Punctuality is the soul of business', decided my mental habit. I thought I could play truant from her and her everlasting lectures on character, but she was on the river and in the wood before me, bringing her barges along or bundling her faggots or calling me in her strong dialect. Among other things, she indicated that the Church was the centre of the village and her calendar the essential year-book of man in nature; Easter was no ideal ceremony but the bright triumph of spring; Advent was in every way the remedy, the hope of those dark and shorn weeks when life was drooping. She also assured me that shoeing horses and baking bread and hitting a cricket-ball were not so simple as they looked, and that we should get on faster if I observed certain points discovered by herself some considerable age before I was thought about. She even compelled me to keep a diary, recording the state of the weather, the news of the day, my private and public life, and my reading; and she saw that this was not skipped. In short it would require a volume to recount all the influences of tradition on the present witness, but it would be the best volume to accompany such attempts at poetry as came in due season. For she governed their sources.

For the matter of the poet's rhythm and versification, tradition is again an unescapable Elizabeth, or, as she has been more familiarly styled, Gammer Gurton or Mother Goose. First of all, there are those mysterious rhythms on which the world goes round and man, body and soul, with it. I shall not go so far as to assert that my latterly unpopular heroine organized those; the tide, the galloping horse, the homeward rooks, the wind in the corn, the pulse of the blood, the travelling cannon-ade of thunder, the play of echo, the tripping of deer, the poising of the hawk-moth—these and the multitude of primeval rhythms besides are older than herself. But she has from a very early date adapted these to the purpose of human utterance fit to be retained in the memory, 'from grave to gay, from lively to severe', and we are as much her disciplined children in this respect as in the fact of our not calling for our lunch with a stone axe in hand. We begin experience to the tune of 'Awake my soul', we close it to the tune of 'Abide with me' or 'O God our help'. We receive before we are aware of it an extraordinary miscellany of verse forms, from the nursery rhyme to the popular success of the music hall. We cannot evade it; our metrical consciousness is traditional. 'Traditional' is not to be translated according to the versifying ambitions or dis-contents of an individual. We may go on, and must go

on, exploring the cave of harmony; the peculiar turn
of each one's fate and insight will require an exactitude
of response in verbal music; but the great series of
metrical inventions which tradition has already evolved
is almost capable of supplying the main rhythm and
cadence for any one of our new instances of poetic
passion. I am not the first by any means to point out
that Gammer Gurton, though a stranger to limited
editions and the disquisitions on prosody, could do
almost anything she liked with a few dozen words of
English.

I cannot avoid quoting some examples of her genius:
'Experiments in Metre. By A Lady of England'—the
original A.L.O.E. They are to be taken, for the
moment, simply in reference to the notion I have been
putting forward on traditional conditions of versecraft.
First, 'The Bouncing Girl':

> What care I how black I be?
> Twenty pounds will marry me;
> If twenty don't, forty shall,
> For I'm my mother's bouncing gal.

Then, 'The Tell-Tale':

> I will tell my own daddy when he comes home
> What little good work my mammy has done;
> She has earnt a penny, spent a groat,
> And a hole is torn in the baby's new coat.

The last two stanzas of 'Giles Collins and Proud Lady
Anna':

> Lady Anna was buried in the east,
>   Giles Collins was buried in the west;
> There grew a lily from Giles Collins
>   That touched Lady Anna's breast, breast,
>   That touched Lady Anna's breast.

There blew a cold north-easterly wind
    And cut this lily in twain
Which never there was seen before,
    And it never will again, again,
    And it never will again.

'Poor Robin' comes with a prophecy of Keats:

The north-wind doth blow
And we shall have snow,
And what will poor Robin do then,
                Poor thing?

He'll sit in a barn
And keep himself warm,
And hide his head under his wing,
                Poor thing.

'Pippen Hill' is Housmanish:

As I was going up Pippen Hill
    Pippen Hill was dirty,
There I met a pretty Miss
    And she dropped me a curtsy.

Little Miss, pretty Miss,
    Blessings light upon you!
If I had half a crown in purse
    I'd spend it all upon you!

'Dame Widdle Waddle':

Old Mother Widdle Waddle jumpt out of bed,
And out at the casement she popt her head
            Crying,
'The house is on fire, the grey goose is dead
And the fox he is come to the town, oh!'

'The Man in the Wilderness' is in that run of verse which
to my sense has always been most translucent, melo-

dious, and natural in the work of Miss Sitwell, who in
our present skirmish comes to the rescue of Experiment:

> The man in the wilderness asked me,
> 'How many strawberries grow in the sea?'
> I answered him, as I thought good;
> 'As many as strawberries grow in the wood.'

And here is the syncopator in 'Hinx Minx';

> Hinx, Minx! the old witch winks,
>   The fat begins to fry:
> There 's nobody at home but jumping Joan
>   And father, mother and I!

The last of these very few of the casual ditties of old
tradition—she merely throws them off for the nursery—
reminds me of the most recent experiment in metre
which I have met with. Mr. J. M. March's boxing-
poem called 'The Set-Up' comes from America, and
since the English edition is 'limited to two thousand
copies' at half a guinea it is plainly considered something conspicuously new in verse. It is on this model:

> The bell hammered,
> Staccato,
> Swift.
> The announcer's arm began to lift.
> He bellowed,
> Mouth wide:
> Turning from side to side:
>
> 'LA-A-DE-EES—AN'
> Gents . . .
> LA-A-DE-EES AN'
> Gents . . .'
> His voice roared out;
> Echoed;
> Immense:

'The NEXT
BOUT
Of the EVENING
Will Be . . .'

'. . . What 's dat he says—?'
'. . . Who—?'
'. . . Don't ask me!'

It may appear odd, but the old lady accompanied the poet to the ringside. The twentieth-century independent is in the tradition.

There remains the gift, the inevitable element of words and turns of phrase, and once more no poet is asked to make something out of nothing. The new taste and the new situation require a fresh composition, but the race has perfected the resources of speech. It is given to few individuals to fabricate new words which become part of our conversation and our feeling, and those individuals are men like Coleridge with a particular philological comprehension, men whose startling life of ideas has been nourished from the beginning in the acquaintance of all types of talk and all literary methods. Immense assurance is needed by one who snubs tradition and her vocabulary and comes forward with his new coinage of quaintnesses and euphemisms. Meanwhile, if ever poets found the mystery of expressive word and idiom ready to their hands, they are the poets of this country. They have only to keep their ears open, whether it is in the town street or the village inn, to make themselves masters of verb, adjective, metaphor, proverbial allusion, and other means of eloquence combining sound and sense like pony and van. Let them copy old Burton of the *Anatomy of Melancholy*, leaning over the bridge at Oxford and shaking his sides at the vigorous dialogues of the bargees. The 'vulgar tongue', as it is called, is a work of genius, and even its violences should make a man desirous of equipping himself for pithy enterprise with the pen rejoice at the imaginative accuracy of old England. The question before the house of bards is not what to concoct, but what to recapture out of the pro-digious word-experience of the Englishman. We have all the linguistic gold that we, and our grandsons and our great-grandsons even more brilliant than we, can keep in beneficial movement.

It is when tradition herself fails, through some com-motion or malady, that we lose sight of the economy of human achievement. When she, by the bad effects of industrial greed and European war, or by half-educa-tion, is not sure of herself, we suffer for it. In the eigh-teenth century the Briton built his house

From Halfpenny's exact designs:

he appeared a trifle ridiculous in his solemnity, but his doors closed quietly, his fireplaces were generous, and his house-front looked out like a square of mild sun-light between his groves and garden walls. Halfpenny's designs costing too much to satisfy a new mania, the Briton turned to plaster and disproportion; and now we have what is fairly described as the architectural obscenity of the vile medleys of tooth-paste and face-cream packages stuck along our highways, 'residences'. Something like this has been allowed to happen, in spite of Sir James Murray and the Fowlers, with the English language. A relaxed generation contents itself, no, glories in a farrago of vapid and dissonant expres-sions, which are applied more or less without alteration to all heads of interest. In this country, which has a world's honour for thoroughness, we see the superficial, and the worst incoherences of that, spreading 'like danger in a wood'. The analphabetism of the counter-feit gives us as a perpetual epithet the valuable indica-tory word 'nice', *e. g.* 'a nice cathedral'; the stirring verb 'mix' ('she doesn't mix'); or 'love' ('I'd love an Austin'). I will not pursue this leafless track, but return from it to the turnpike road of tradition, and ask whether the poets will stand for clear and various communication or the opposite. If they wish for an antidote to idiocy and an inspiration for sound re-creation, let them go to a farmer's ordinary, a scientist's lecture, or an eigh-teenth-century schoolbook.

In fact, I will recite for them a passage, every way accordant with my own convictions on the nature of poetic inheritance and progress, from a schoolbook published in 1748. Even the title-page exhibits a seasoned discrimination of language which makes it a model even to the most visionary;

THE
PRECEPTOR:
containing
A General Course of Education
wherein
THE FIRST PRINCIPLES
of
POLITE LEARNING
are laid down
In a way most suitable for trying the GENIUS,
and advancing the
Instruction of YOUTH.

When we come to the 'Lesson on Poetry', we may take

with us the trivial and undistinguishing cant which a hundred modern reviews of verse cause to seem the only possibility, but it will soon fly like a mist before this sturdy sunlight:

'Tho' Invention be the Mother of Poetry, yet this Child is like all others, born naked, and must be nourished with Care, cloath'd with Exactness and Elegance, educated with Industry, instructed with Art, improved by Application, corrected with Severity, and accomplished with Labour and with Time, before it arrives at any great Perfection or Growth. 'Tis certain, that no Composition requires so many Ingredients, or of more different Sorts, than this; nor that to excel in any Qualities, there are necessary so many Gifts of Nature, and so many Improvements of Learning and of Art. For there must be an universal Genius, of great Compass, as well as great Elevation. There must be a sprightly Imagination or Fancy, fertile in a thousand Productions, ranging over infinite Ground, piercing into every Corner, and by the Light of that true poetical Fire, discovering a thousand little Bodies or Images in the World, and Similitudes among them, unseen to common Eyes, and which could not be discover'd without the Rays of that Sun. Besides the Heat of Invention and Liveliness of Wit, there must be the Coldness of Good Sense, and Soundness of Judgment, to distinguish between Things and Conceptions, which at first sight, or upon short Glance, seem alike; to chuse among infinite Productions of Wit and Fancy, which are worth preserving and cultivating, and which are better stifled in the Birth, or thrown away when they are born, as not worth bringing up.

'Without the Forces of Wit, all Poetry is flat and languishing; without the succours of Judgment, 'tis wild and extravagant. The true Wonder of Poesy is, that such Contraries must meet to compose it; a Genius both penetrating and solid; in Expression both Delicacy and Force; and the Frame or Fabric of a true Poem, must have something both

F

sublime and just, amazing and agreeable. There must be
a great Agitation of Mind to invent, a great Calm to judge
and correct; there must be upon the same Tree, and at the
same time, both Flower and Fruit. To work up this Metal
into exquisite Figure, there must be employed the Fire,
the Chissel, and the File. There must be a general Knowledge both of Nature and the Arts; and to go to the lowest
that can be, there are required Genius, Judgment and Application; for without this last, all the rest will not serve
Turn, and none ever was a great Poet that applied himself
much to anything else.'

Such is the style in which our tradition discusses an
abstract subject, with a firmness of words never failing
in aptitude, with a dramatic instancy yet no extrava-
gance, and when a modern Englishman sees what he
wishes to propound and has acquired that readiness of
diction, he may go farther and introduce what novelty
he will; he can be trusted not to use dynamite or cheap
scent. Let us also refresh our memories in respect of
tradition's acute sense of description, given an external
object. We have lately heard Mr. D. H. Lawrence as a
poet of natural history; he has won the bewildering
superlatives of Mr. Middleton Murry for such experiments as his poem to the baby tortoise, and his wor-
shipper, quoting the lines

> Alone, small insect,
> Tiny bright eye,
> Slow one,

observes that the piece 'is lovely with a passion that all
the sons of women have it in them to understand'. I
may be singular, but somehow I am still looking for the
tortoise. The trouble is that I was made acquainted
with tradition's ability to 'notice such things'. And I

find actually more of poetry in, for example, the curt observations of Thomas Pennant on animals.

'The cat, a useful but deceitful domestic: when pleased, purrs and moves its tail: when angry, spits, hisses, strikes with its foot: in walking, draws in its claws: drinks little: is fond of fish: the female very salacious; a piteous, jarring, squalling lover: the natural enemy of mice: watches them with great gravity: does not always reject vegetables: washes its face with its fore feet at the approach of a storm: sees by night: its eyes shine in the dark: always lights on its feet: proverbially tenacious of life: very cleanly; hates wet: is fond of perfumes; *marum, valerian, catmint*. The unaccountable antipathy of multitudes! beloved by the *Mahometans*: *Maillet*, who says that the cats of *Aegypt* are very beautiful, adds, that the inhabitants build hospitals for them.'

I have taken this quite ordinary example of traditional writing in order to illustrate the straightforward force of the language when it is modestly practised. I am only on the fringe of an immense subject, which may be comprised in few: new strength of diction can be best produced by a mature intelligence in the extant resources both printed and oral.

Tradition is not perfect, and may sometimes have a dead hand. But though she approves and supports many things which could be vastly improved—though, according to an old French song,

> Hypocrisy and suave intrigue,
> Successful impudence and lying,
> Lawlessness with law in league,
> Talent in the gutter dying—
> Cant,
> Rant
> And superstition
> Are the favourites of Tradition—

still her merits far outweight her faults. Viewed altogether, she is the edifice of experience, the constitution
of our society, and the test of the future. In the sphere
of the arts, she may appear as a grim Johnsonian critic,
but she will listen to genius, because she knows that
genius has listened to her though he may not have been
aware of it. She herself is astonished and aggrieved
when a steam-engine advances, leaving the driver of
the Norwich stage-coach snapping his whip at the
posturing smoke; or when the broadcasting programme
makes her lament the days of the silent evenings, inter-
rupted by the old village bells; but she sleeps on it, and
before long decides that the times are as good as they
were. Her sentiment can never be outraged by what is
shaped and revised according to the laws of evolution;
she has only to look at the poster on the Underground,
setting forth the Londoner's means of transit through
the ages, to feel at home in 1929 as in 1829; she may
see even her stage-coach, disguised as new necessity
demands, gliding out from Paddington. It is little
different in the province of innovation and experiment
on the part of the musician, the painter, and the poet.
We cannot, unless we are creatures of the cave, the
tripod, and the oracle, see clearly the works of art
which she will choose to preserve out of the swarm of
endeavours endlessly surrounding her; but the past can
assure us that in all that is destined to survive there will
be found no hysterical, miraculous, demon-begotten
departure from the past. The leap forward will have
been made possible by a steady and accurately judged
jumping-off place. In its preparation there needs no
feverish anxiety or palaver about the future style of
civilization. On this ground many modern talents

come to grief; the terror of seeming five minutes behind next Friday distracts and exhausts. Those with things to say spend their enthusiasm in distorting the ways of saying them. So a village boy with a telegram to deliver trains a goat to accompany him, with a satchel round its neck, and in that the telegram, if the goat has not contrived to eat it on the road.

I have said that the past can assure us how far poetical discovery and adventure is related to what was previously ascertained and imparted. Poetry is a family, and her genealogical tree may be investigated with patience and reward. Sometimes a particular branch of this family is remarkable for a rich succession of 'likenesses' in difference. If we trace Virgil or Milton through posterity, we shall be busy for many years; from their fountain-heads (yet those fountains were supplied from their predecessors in usual measure) many a fine stream of verse went its own way through the personalities and emotions of other poets, long since recognized as masters. I should like to close my wandering thoughts on the newness of poetical action that is always implicit in a devotion to former excellence, with references to the work of some whose genius is unmistakably original and kindling with revelation. Time allows us now a perspective of such a phenomenon as Blake. We know his hand, 'the trick of that voice we do well remember'. We see him single in the field, or attended only by his angels. But poetically he is not unaccompanied; the Elizabethan dramatists with their lyrical enjoyments and splendid panoramas of fate and mortality are there. A figure who might not be expected in such company is there also. Watts's Hymns are no longer the common knowledge of England, but

in Blake's time they were so, and he transfused their
celestial moments into his own visionary illuminings.

> Come, lead me to some lofty shade,
>   Where turtles moan their loves;
> Tall shadows were for lovers made
>   And grief becomes the groves . . .
>
> Jesus! the God of might and love
>   New-moulds our limbs of cumbrous clay;
> Quick as seraphic flames we move,
>   Active and young and fair as they.
>
> Our airy feet with unknown flight
>   Swift as the motions of desire
> Run up the hills of heavenly light
>   And leave the weltering world in fire . . .

There are many stanzas like these in Isaac Watts, which
have their soft but clear echoes in Blake's lyrics.

Coleridge again is known as a poet new in his own
day and new in ours; he was continually experimenting,
and in metre his experiments set free a countless host
of melodies; almost, one might say, a fresh prosody.
But even this magician did not experiment without the
help of his old friend Tradition. We do not take away
any of the life and spring of his

> Never, believe me,
> Appear the immortals,

when we realize that the origin of this freedom is a
German lyric; nor when we know that a German folk-
song underlies 'Something Childish but very Natural'
is the charm broken. Repeating with pleasure the
stanza beginning

> Once again, sweet Willow, lave thee!
> Why stays my Love?

we are repeating what was suggested by the Welsh air
'All through the night'. Even 'Christabel' is rhythmi-
cally a renovation and enrichment of nursery-rhyme
measure. And there is that apparently unprecedented
and inimitable poem 'Kubla Khan'—from the air, from
the wood beyond the world? Let Coleridge himself
give his statement on the genesis of 'Kubla Khan':

'In the summer of the year 1797, the Author, then in ill
health, had retired to a lonely farm house between Porlock
and Linton, on the Exmoor confines of Somerset and
Devonshire. In consequence of a slight indisposition, an
anodyne had been prescribed, from the effect of which he
fell asleep in his chair at the moment that he was reading
the following sentence, or words of the same substance, in
"Purchas's Pilgrimage": "Here the Khan Kubla com-
manded a palace to be built, and a stately garden thereunto:
and thus ten miles of fertile ground were enclosed with
a wall." The author continued for about three hours in
a profound sleep, at least of the external senses, during
which time he has the most vivid confidence, that he could
not have composed less than from two to three hundred
lines; if that indeed can be called composition in which all
the images rose up before him as things, with a parallel
production of the correspondent expressions, without any
sensation or consciousness of effort.'

Summertime in the country, to be sure, and a solitary
place, and the anodyne, and Purchas, and the genius of
dreams, are all felt as presences in the ensuing fantasy
which surpasses all our fantasies; but that is not all.
For rhythmical sequences and surprises, for verbal
music and ideal scenery, Coleridge's secret recollection
of two poems by William Collins (themselves descended
in some characteristics from Dryden) must partly have
our thanks. Those poems are the 'Ode on the Passions',

with its 'prophetic sounds' of the 'war-denouncing trumpet', its music of instrument and nature.

Through glades and glooms the mingled measure stole;

and the 'Ode on the Poetical Character', which Coleridge honours in an early preface, and

> Where tangled round the jealous steep,
> Strange shades o'erbrow the vallies deep,
> And holy genii guard the rock,
> Its glooms embrown, its springs unlock.

Without pausing to elaborate this—I imagine that is all done in Professor Livingston Lowes' 'Road to Xanadu'—I hasten on to find Milton's great ghost and oriental vision joining in the symphony, whether in the reminiscence of

> Southward through Eden went a river large,
> Nor changed his course, but through the shaggy hill
> Passed underneath ingulphed,

to 'rise a fresh fountain and with many a rill Water the glade'; or of other, or all his landscapes of romance and wonder.

In pointing out some of the contacts between Coleridge's voyage of discovery and the ports of tradition, I must not be mistaken as belittling the splendour of his newness or as being blind to the individuality of the poem. Coleridge was necessary and only Coleridge. But (to paraphrase Browning's not very beautiful question) could Coleridge grow up without porridge? It may be objected to tradition that when her bewildering child presented her with 'Kubla Khan' she struck him in the face. Enter, in short, the *Quarterly Review* for September 1816. *Quarterly* speaks:

'It was in the year 1797, and in the summer season.

Mr. Coleridge was in bad health;—the particular disease
is not given; but the careful reader will form his own con-
jectures. . . . In that farm-house, he had a slight indisposition, and had taken an anodyne, which threw him into
a deep sleep in his chair (whether after dinner or not he
omits to state . . .). The lines here given smell strongly,
it must be owned, of the anodyne; and, but that an under-
dose of a sedative produces contrary effects, we should
inevitably have been lulled by them into forgetfulness of all
things. Perhaps a dozen more lines such as the following
would reduce the most irritable of critics to inaction.'

And so on—'utterly destitute of value', 'not a ray of
genius'. In spite of this bad beginning Tradition had
to admit 'Kubla' to the album, and presently the two
got on famously together; so now we may stand looking
for a 'Kubla Khan' of our days, and if our poets are
as traditional as Coleridge we may receive one.

EXPERIMENT IN POETRY

By EDITH SITWELL

WORDSWORTH in an essay Supplementary to Preface, 1815, writes:

'Of genius the only proof is in the act of doing well what is worthy to be done, and what was never done before; of genius, in the fine arts, the only infallible sign is the widening of the sphere of human sensibility, for the delight, honour, and benefit of human nature. Genius is the introduction of the new element to the intellectual universe; or, if that be not allowed, it is the application of powers to objects on which they had not before been exercised, or the employment of them in such a manner as to produce effects hitherto unknown. What is all this but an advance or a conquest, made by the soul of the poet? Is it to be supposed that the reader can make progress of this kind like an Indian prince or general stretched on his palaquin, and borne by his slaves? No; he is invigorated and inspired by his leader, in order that he may exert himself; for he cannot proceed in quiescence, he cannot be carried like a dead weight, there-force, to create taste is to call forth and bestow power, of which knowledge is the effect; and *there* lies the true difficulty.'

It should be remembered, and is remembered, that practically every poet of importance since the time of Shakespeare has defended innovations and experiments in prefaces and in essays. Ben Jonson has done so, Milton has done so, to mention only two early poets. There is not time, or I could quote to you passages from these and almost every other poet, all stating the necessity of experiment. At one time there were arguments as to the advisability of rhyming—this being regarded as an innovation. Then there were arguments about the novelty of blank verse. The truth is, that the great poet is, in almost every case, both a traditionalist and an experimentalist. He does not forget the discoveries made and the examples shown by his great predecessors, but, at the same time, he *must* bring some freshness into the language, some technical innovation, some new discovery of the world of sight or sound, else he is merely an echo, and will not take his place among his predecessors.

There has been no great poet who has not made discoveries and experiments in the material, the clay (let us call it) of his art. Alexander Pope, for instance— he springs to my mind because I am writing a book about him at the moment—Alexander Pope who was one of the greatest of our poets, made numerous discoveries on the effect that texture has on rhythm. Sir Leslie Stephen has been insensitive enough to say that Pope found the heroic couplet ready made for him. Nothing could be more falsified, as a statement. Within the rigid limits of the heroic couplet, he succeeded in producing an extraordinary variation, due to nothing but texture, since the beat of the heroic couplet was unchanged. The subtlety was amazing. To a sensitive ear if the hearer had not an expert knowledge, the rhythm of that part of *The Rape of the Lock* which deals with the Sylphs and the rhythm of the *Dunciad* would appear to be different. Yet both are written in flawless heroic couplets. The effect is gained by the incredibly delicate labials and sibilants in the one, and the heavy, double consonanted words in the other.

This is particularly interesting to me, because most

of the technical experiments which are being made to-day are experiments in the effect of texture on rhythm. Those experiments are of a much more violent order than those made by Pope—for violence is necessary in order to convey the spirit of the time—but the basis of those experiments is the same. If you ask why rhythms have become more violent, the answer is: that this is an age of machinery—a wild race for time, confined within limits that are at once mad and circumscribed. Try to get out, and you knock your head against the walls of materialism. This state of things is mirrored in modern syncopated dance music, which removes music from the world of inspiration, which evolves itself organically from the inner need of the artist, and brings it into the world of machinery where form is superimposed as a logical idea. There is no time or space in which to dream. It is because of this that in those poems which deal with the world crumbling to dust, with materialism building monstrous shapes out of the deadened dust, I, for one, use the most complicated dance rhythms which could be found, or else syncopated rhythms which are not dance rhythms. I experiment, for instance, in the different effect that two one-syllabled words and one two-syllabled word have on rhythm in heightening or slowing the speed. Now I am afraid I am going to quote a poem of mine, not out of egoism, or because I underrate the poems of other writers, but merely because it is a useful blackboard example of the point which I wish to make.

Fox Trot

Old Sir Faulk
    Tall as a stork,
Before the honeyed fruits of dawn were ripe, would walk

And stalk with a gun
The reynard-coloured sun
Among the pheasant-feathered corn the unicorn has torn,
    forlorn the
Smock-faced sheep
Sit and sleep
Periwigged as William and Mary, weep:
'Sally, Mary, Mattie, what's the matter, why cry?'
The huntsman and the reynard-coloured sun and I sigh.
'Oh the nursery-maid Meg
With a leg like a peg
Chased the feathered dreams like hens and when they laid
    an egg
In the sheepskin
Meadows
Where
The serene King James would steer
Horse and hounds, then he
In the shade of a tree
Picked it up as spoil to boil for nursery tea,' said the mourners.
    In the
Corn, towers strain
Feathered tall as a crane,
And whistling down the feathered rain, old Noah goes again—
An old dull mome
With a head like a pome,
Seeing the world as a bare egg
Laid by the feathered air; Meg
Would beg three of these
For the nursery teas
Of Japhet, Shem, and Ham; she gave it
Underneath the trees
Where the boiling
                    Water
                    Hissed
Like the goose-king's feathered daughter—kissed

Pot and pan and copper kettle
Put upon their proper mettle
Lest the Flood, the Flood, the Flood begin again through
    these.

In this poem you find the effect of rhyme and texture
on rhythm. The effect of the length or shortness of notes
in music are got by the contrast of the dark heavy
sounds of *o* in 'old', *ir* in 'Sir', and also the dark
sounds of tall and stork, stork being the darker of the
two, but both being almost yet not quite assonances—
these give a kind of ground rhythm, interspersed with
the lighter, quicker, more frivolous-sounding double-
syllabled and treble-syllabled words, 'reynard-coloured
sun, pheasant-feathered, periwigged—all of these assonances where the 'ea' sound in these particular words
is very short instead of long. In this poem, too, we see
the different effect single-syllabled and double-syllabled
words have on rhythm. Single-syllabled words are
much slower than double-syllabled words as we shall
see if we compare the lines

> Smock-faced sheep
> Sit and sleep

with lines containing double or treble-syllabled words,
ending with one or more one-syllabled words:

> Periwigged as William and Mary, weep:

or

> 'Sally, Mary, Mattie, what's the matter, why cry?'
> The huntsman and the reynard-coloured sun and I sigh.

We see from this, also, the violent effect that rhymes
placed close together have upon rhythm;

> Why cry?
> I sigh.

This gives the effect of two leaps into the air. We see, also, the effect that internal rhymes contained in one line, but *not* placed together, have upon rhythm.

Among the pheasant-feathered corn the unicorn has torn,
    forlorn the, &c. . . .

These have exactly the opposite effect of that gained by rhymes placed immediately together. The repetition keeps the rhythm almost super-smooth.

See, also, the effect words that are not quite an assonance yet not quite a dissonance have on rhythm, when placed at regular intervals in a line:

Tall as a stork.

The longest rest falls on 'stork', and this would not have been so pointed if the other word were not a slight hardly perceptible discord.

Wilfred Owen, who would, I feel sure, have been a great poet if he had lived, was making experiments in the effect of assonances and dissonances—but more from an emotional point of view than from a rhythmical point of view, since he used them in slow-moving poems, such as his great poem 'Strange Meeting', written a month before he was killed, where this technique gives the effect of terrible gloom, despair, and weariness, yet majesty in its slow movement. I will quote the shorter version, because the complete poem is too long.

Earth's wheels run oiled with blood. Forget we that.
Let us lie down and dig ourselves in thought.
Beauty is yours and you have mastery,
Wisdom is mine, and I have mystery.
We two will stay behind and keep our troth.
Let us forego men's minds that are brutes' natures,
Let us not sup the blood which some say nurtures,

Be we not swift with swiftness of the tigress.
Let us break ranks from those who trek from progress.
Miss we the march of this retreating world
Into old citadels that are not walled.
Let us lie out and hold the open truth.
Then when their blood hath clogged the chariot wheels
We will go up and wash them from deep wells.
What though we sink from men as pitchers falling
Many shall raise us up to be their filling
Even from wells we sunk too deep for war
And fitted by brows that bled where no wounds were.

Now, throughout this wonderful poem, Owen gained his effects (with one or two exceptions) by using dissonances with the larger-sounding vowels at the *beginning* of each couplet. The use of the *shorter*-sounding vowels in the second line of each couplet gives the effect of weariness, of being too tired to hold on. In other words, he nearly always uses Falling Feet, as they are called.

Baudelaire has a wonderful quatrain with dissonances in his 'Bénédiction', though the effect is completely different.

> Elle ravale ainsi l'écume de sa haine,
> Et, ne comprenant pas les desseins éternels,
> Elle-même prépare au fond de la Géhenne
> Les bûchers consacrés aux crimes maternels.

Now the effect of that is terrible in its ferocity, and most extraordinary from a technical point of view. The fact that 'haine' has long double vowels gives the effect of a kind of tiger's roar, or of a roar from all the throats in hell—I don't know how else to describe it. Then we get the double-syllabled 'Géhenne' which starts with the same sound and then—because it *is* double-syllabled— has an appalling *breaking* effect, with the second syllable with its short dull *n*-sound, giving the effect of some-body clasping this hellish passion, shrinking away to the breast, out of the sight of day. I don't know any-thing comparable to it.

It is interesting to contrast Owen's poem with Tennyson's 'Tears, Idle Tears', which is not only one of the loveliest short lyrics in the English language, but is, I sometimes imagine, the origin of these speculations.

I shall quote it, although every one knows it well, to prove my contention.

> Tears, idle tears, I know not what they mean,
> Tears from the depth of some divine despair
> Rise in the heart, and gather to the eyes,
> In looking on the happy Autumn-fields,
> And thinking of the days that are no more.
>
> Fresh as the first beam glittering on a sail,
> That brings our friends up from the underworld,
> Sad as the last which reddens over one
> That sinks with all we love below the verge;
> So sad, so fresh, the days that are no more.
>
> Ah, sad and strange as in dark summer dawns
> The earliest pipe of half-awaken'd birds
> To dying ears, when unto dying eyes
> The casement slowly grows a glimmering square;
> So sad, so strange, the days that are no more.
>
> Dear as remember'd kisses after death,
> And sweet as those by hopeless fancy feign'd
> On lips that are for others; deep as love,
> Deep as first love, and wild with all regret;
> O Death in Life, the days that are no more.

G

This unrhymed poem is not in blank verse—the effect is very different to that of Owen's poem, not only because the metre is different, but also because, whereas Owen often ends his lines with a double-syllabled word where the accent falls on the first syllable, in short, with a falling foot, thus giving the unutterable feeling of weariness, Tennyson, in his divine poem, ends nearly always with a one-syllabled word, or, where he uses a double-syllabled word, it is always one where the syllables are equal—'despair', 'regret', and when he uses a treble-syllabled word, it is where the first and last syllables are equal, 'underworld'. Now, though this poem does not rhyme, the vowels in the words at the end of the lines have a most peculiar effect—witness the poignancy of 'mean', and after two lines, the assonance of 'fields'—the lifting sound of the word 'eyes' and the dark sound of the word 'more': all this has a beautiful effect, and must raise many speculations in the poet's mind.

I hope I have not wearied you with these technical matters. We will now pass to others. To put it in a nutshell—one of the principal aims of the new poets is to increase consciousness. The purpose of art and literature is not to educate us into a state where, like Villiers de l'Isle Adam's hero Axël, our servants must do our living for us. It is, rather, to give us increased vitality and a more passionate sense of life and power for living. We do not try to force our way of seeing upon the people. What we try to do is to give the people their own way of seeing—to remove fear. We explain that there are a thousand aspects of even the most ordinary subject, and that we see this subject in such and such a way. This will help each person, in his turn, to arrive at an individual view and idea of this object. All this enriches life, it adds experience: not only that; it will eventually increase the consciousness of the race.

One of the reasons why the pioneers in the arts are so much disliked is that the public have got into the way of thinking that man has always seen as he sees now. This is wrong. Not only has he seen with different eyes, but it is impossible that we shall all see alike at the present time, although the crowd would prefer uniformity of sight. The modernist artist gives us the great chance of exerting an individuality in seeing. The older beauty, the beauty of the Old Masters, is in the beauty of species and of mass—the new beauty is highly individualized and separate. The modern artist is not concerned with things in the mass, he is passionately interested in the fulfilling of the destinies of the single individuals that make up the mass—whether these individuals are men, or leaves, or waves of the sea. The great quality of the old masters in all the arts is force, used in the scientific sense of the term—the binding together of the molecules of the world. That is partly what made their sense of design so tremendous. The great quality of the modern masters is an explosive energy—the separating up of the molecules—exploring the possibilities of the atom. This is at once the quality and the danger of pioneer poetry. The aim of the modernist poets—the constant aim—is to reconcile this necessity of exploring the possibilities of the atom, with the necessity for logical design and form. The primary needs in poetry to-day are a greater expressiveness, a greater formality, and a return to rhetoric (good rhetoric, be it understood). Expressiveness and rhetoric mean almost but not quite the same thing. Bad rhetoric, by which I mean superimposed rhetoric—images which are meaningless and unrelated to the material and shape of the poem—is bad poetry. It was bad rhetoric which produced Stephen Phillips. But, with the exception of Wordsworth, the unceasing enemy of rhetoric, all our greatest poetry has been created, partly, by its rhetoric. Examine Milton for the truth of this. We must fear the debilitated state and lavered vitality which is shown by the outcry for under-statement, for quietness, for neutral tints in poetry.

Another need in poetry is a higher sense of balance between the two components of a work of art—the spiritual side and the physical side. As regards form, there is, on the one hand, too much lolling over the borders of freedom into vacancy, on the other hand, too much tight-lacing and revulsion against growth. On this subject Mr. Ezra Pound, in an article on Dolmetsch, said: 'Any work of art is a compound of freedom and of order. It is perfectly obvious that art hangs between chaos on the one hand and mechanics on the other. A pedantic insistence upon detail tends to drive out major form. A firm hold on major form makes for a freedom of detail.'

This is true. The proof of originality in a work of art is to produce personality in the bare line. At the same time there has grown up, nowadays, an almost maniacal hatred of beauty in detail—a loathing of imagery. Persons who are incapable of perceiving the relationship between any two objects and who are, consequently, incapable of perceiving the design of the world, refer to images as bric-à-brac. Naturally, the greatest poetry is not that on which the images are encrusted in such a way that they could tumble off without the design being disturbed: but that in which you cannot separate the image from the structure. Flesh and hair make the living form more beautiful, you may have observed, however elegant the structure of the bone may be. But English poetry to-day is a positive charnel-house of deformed and strengthless skeletons on the one hand, and on the other, a ware-house full of rolls of cheap linoleum—all this because of fear—fear of life, fear of madness, fear of free verse, though, as Mr. Eliot has pointed out, 'the term is a loose one . . . any verse is called free by people whose ears are unaccustomed to it'.

Every now and then a great outcry arises from the people and the press—a complaint that modern art is mad—in other words, irrational. I can only hope that the people are right. All great art contains an element of the irrational. One might almost say that art is the irrational spirit contained in a structure of the purest and most logical form. Without that logical form or architecture the irrational does, of course, become lunacy. The irrational spirit in logical form produced such creators as Shakespeare, Michael Angelo, da Vinci, Beethoven. On the other hand, the logical spirit in irrational form produced such creators as Mr. Gossip of the *Daily Sketch*, the sur-realistes, all the little English and American would-be poets living in Paris, Mr. Desmond McCarthy, Dr. Frank Crane of the 'Tonic Talks'. Art is magic, not logic. This craze for the logical spirit in irrational shape is part of the present harmful mania for uniformity—in an age when women try to abolish the difference between their aspect and aims and those of men, in an age when the edict has gone forth for the abolition of personality, for the abolition of faces—which are practically extinct. It is because of this hatred of personality that the crowd, in its uniformity, dislikes artists endued with an individual vision.

Yet when we come to consider the realm of new poetry, or of newness, and consequently strangeness—in any of the arts—let us remember that the irritation felt by people contemplating this newness has been felt by each generation towards the pioneer artists of their time. It is an irritation which is, however painful to the artist, in some ways natural to mankind. Yet it is obvious that it would not have been useful for Christopher Columbus to discover a potato patch in Spain, nor would it have been useful for Newton to discover the truths found by Galileo; and this applies equally to the arts. What an artist is for is to tell us what we see but do not know that we see. His duty is not to repeat to us, word for word, exactly what we, our fathers, and grandfathers prattled about from the cradle. But a great many people are over-tired when they have passed the age of twenty, and they don't want to be made to travel to Christopher Columbus's discoveries, or to hear the truths that were found by Newton. They are inclined to laugh at the unknown, to mock at its strange fantastic appearance, forgetting that this queer irritating substance when it becomes, as it will become automatically, a classic, will be so known, that future generations will take its beauty for granted without worrying about it. Many people say, as they have always said about contemporary work of any importance: 'These discoveries bring no great message to mankind.' How do they know? Every message is not concerned with sentimental relations between people. That is not the only aspect with which poetry is concerned. And the aspects of modern poetry are very varied. It is absurd to pretend that modernist poets have no love for humanity and are not interested in humanity.

A great many of the poems by the most advanced school—those poems which seem strangest to us—deal with the growth of consciousness—or with consciousness awakening from sleep. Sometimes you find a consciousness that has been like that of a blind person, becoming aware, intensely aware, of the nature of a tree, or of a flower, or of the way in which rain hangs or falls from objects, for the first time, and, seeing that nature, guessing, however dimly, that there is a reason, a design, somewhere outside their present state of consciousness. You find the animal state of consciousness, shaping itself from within, beginning to evolve shape out of its thick black blot of darkness. For with the development of shape out of chaos, with the power to grasp something physically, consciousness begins. It is that shaping process that you find in this poem of Marianne Moore's— a poem about an elephant.

Black Earth

Openly, yes,
with the naturalness
    of the hippopotamus or the alligator
    when it climbs out on the bank to experience the

sun, I do these
things which I do, which please
    no one but myself. Now I breathe and now I am sub-
    merged; the blemishes stand up and shout when the
      object

in view was a
renaissance; shall I say
    the contrary? The sediment of the river which
    encrusts my joints, makes me very gray but I am used
to it, it may
remain there; do away
    with it and I am myself done away with, for the
    patina of circumstance can but enrich what was
there to begin
with. This elephant skin
    which I inhabit, fibred over like the shell of
    the coco-nut, this piece of black glass through which
      no light
can filter—cut
into checkers by rut
    upon rut of unpreventable experience—
    it is a manual of the peanut-tongued and the
hairy-toed. Black
but beautiful, my back
    is full of the history of power. Of power? What
    is powerful and what is not? My soul shall never
be cut into
by a wooden spear; through-
    out childhood to the present time, the unity of
    life and death has been expressed by the circumference
described by my
trunk; nevertheless, I
    perceive feats of strength to be inexplicable after
    all; and I am on my guard; external poise, it
has its centre
well-nurtured—we know
    where—in pride, but spiritual poise, it has its centre
      where?
    my ears are sensitized to more than the sound of

the wind. I see
and I hear, unlike the
    wandlike body of which one hears so much, which
      was made
    to see and not to see; to hear and not to hear;

that tree trunk without
roots, accustomed to shout
     its own thoughts to itself like a shell, maintained intact
    by one who knows what strange pressure of the
      atmosphere; that

spiritual
brother to the coral
    plant, absorbed into which, the equable sapphire light
    becomes a nebulous green. The I of each is to

the I of each,
a kind of fretful speech
    which sets a limit on itself; the elephant is?
    black earth preceded by a tendril? It is to that

phenomenon
the above formation,
    translucent like the atmosphere—a cortex merely—
    that on which darts cannot strike decisively the first

time, a substance
needful as an instance
    of the indestructibility of matter; it
    has looked at the electricity and at the earth-

quake and is still
here; the name means thick.   Will
    depth be depth, thick skin be thick, to one who can
      see no
    beautiful element of unreason under it?

To me, that poem is not a first-rate one: I do not say
it is quite first-rate. I admit it is fearfully obscure. But

notice how admirably her technique in this case is fitted to the subject. It conveys the great lumbering gait, and, though the lines are short, the huge size of the subject. And this is done by a technical device which Miss Moore uses a thousand times in other poems, to which it is entirely unsuitable—the trick of ending lines with such words as 'of', 'and', or 'a', indeed, even the trick of ending the line in the middle of the word. In other poems of hers, this habit becomes a maddening trick, and, so far as I know, means nothing. The poem is, as Miss Moore would say, about the indestructibility of matter, but it is matter in which, owing to the power of lifting, consciousness is fumbling for the light. 'Black earth preceded by a tendril.' It is an interesting poem, though I do not find the whole of it beautiful. 'Black Earth' seems to me to illustrate at once the virtues and the vices of modernist poetry.

That is one state of consciousness. Sometimes, in these poems, you find a terrible groping animal consciousness—a consciousness which knows only the flowering and urge of its own hot blood and desires, and, through this, its relationship to other material aspects of the world. You find this in a poem by another poet 'Dark Song', where the dissonances which end the lines in the place of rhymes give the discontent of the subject, its groping in the blackness, without finding what it is groping for. May I ask you to notice the curious effect that the alternation of dull muted *r*'s and sounded *r*'s have in this poem. They give the effect of the hoarse voice of an animal. Out of the fourteen lines, only four are not built upon this structure of muted and sounded *r*'s. The other curious technical effect of lifting and sinking is gained by the vowel sounds—'flames', 'chain',

&c. This is meant to give the impression of pure animal nature becoming for the moment sharpened by protesting—trying, subconsciously, to become something different.

> The fire is furry as a bear
> And the flames purr . . .
> The dark bear rambles in his chain
> Captive to cruel men
> Through the dark and hairy wood.
> The maid sighed: 'All my blood
> Is animal. They thought I sat
> Like a household cat
> When through the dark woods rambled I.
> Oh, if my blood would die.'
> The fire had a bear's fur . . .
> It heard and knew . . .
> The dark earth furry as a bear
> Grumbled too.

In this poem the poet was not saying that the fire has the shape of an animal: but that in the fire can be found the foreshadowing and beginning of animal life—the flame, which is the spirit, the animal density and blackness, which is coal, and which resembles the furry coat of a bear—and the intermittent sound of the flame, which one day will be the voice of the animal. In fact the poem speaks of the beginning of things, and of primitive nature, before it developed the spirit. Sometimes again you get this animal consciousness knowing its own segregation and loneliness—cut off from the outer world by the lack of that higher consciousness which alone can bring us to those correspondences, as Swedenborg has said, whereby men may speak with angels. A poet comes along and tells us something new.

A person who is not a poet says: 'I do not see things like that.' Of course he doesn't. If he did, either he would be a poet too, or the poet wouldn't be a poet. If the person who is *not* a poet says; 'But I *do* see things as Wordsworth and Keats saw them'—the answer to that is (*a*) that he most certainly does not, and (*b*) that of course he *thinks* he does, because he is living a hundred years after Wordsworth and Keats, and so he has got used to them: whereas he is a contemporary of the poet with whom he has just disagreed and so has not got used to him.

I scarcely need to tell you that all pioneer poets— even such poets as Wordsworth and Keats—have been disagreed with during their lifetime. When, therefore, we are told by a person who is not a poet, that he sees things as Wordsworth or as Keats saw them, we may with justice ask if Wordsworth and that person would have seen eye to eye during Wordsworth's lifetime. The name of Wordsworth could not be mentioned until he was between fifty and sixty without an outburst of vulgar nature from the press. It is not the slightest use for reviewers to fly into a temper and say that it is only the mad artists of to-day who are roughly treated by the crowd. For it can be proved that such treatment, varied by heart-breaking neglect, has been meted out to every artist of importance since the time of Shakespeare. But the people who attack artists to-day are not the real critics but the gossip-writers of certain papers. I beg of you not to be misled or turned against us by the exceedingly foolish young men and women who are writing feeble-minded imitations of modernist poems in verse which is neither free verse nor anything else. These ridiculous efforts are not the fault of the real poets. And now I am going to make some very bad-tempered remarks with which I am sure you will sympathize. Any artist who is doing pioneer work in these days has a terrible amount to contend with; and the dangers to the future of literature come less from dull writers and uninspired critics, than from the terrible little amateurs, the little chic nonsense writers, both French, English, and American, living in Paris. These little people, who, whilst pretending to be modernist, are in reality only repeating the back-chat of twenty years ago about free verse, do not realize (a) that the people who are doing work of any importance in poetry to-day are returning to classicism of structure, as a protest against anarchism, and (b) that free verse has just as much organic form (form arising from the properties of the material) as any other verse. The verse these people write is merely shapeless and flabby magazine verse with the meaning left out. During the existence of a silly paper called *Secession*, the editors, for reasons only known to themselves, sent out a specimen of every number. The contributors gave themselves frightful airs, and thought they were great poets and pioneers and goodness knows what. This is a specimen of their verse. I am not exaggerating. I have copied it out for you.

In a Restaurant

You are a sweet girl and I must leave you to pay the waiter.
You are a sweet girl, and I will give you a bunch of narcissus.
You are a sweet girl, and I will chew your ear.

Compare that nonsense with Mr. Eliot's free verse, and you will see the difference between the false and the true. Free verse has to have just as much organic form, form arising out of the properties of the material, as any other kind of verse. In fact, I return to my previous statement, that art is the irrational spirit in a logical form.

I am aware that when I said, earlier in this lecture, that the finest poetry has an element of the irrational, I said a dangerous thing. But I am assuming that poetry should be written by poets, and not by persons who are not poets. Let us see the difference. I will read you part of a poem by a man who, in my opinion, is one of the greatest poets now writing in our language—this fragment will show how we are returning to this much-to-be-desired state, this strange atmosphere of music, like that of the state of the poem 'Kubla Khan'. It tells no story, nor does it convey any philosophical message, though it speaks of the material and physical world at war. It is just pure poetry—a few lines from a long poem. These few lines can give no impression of the greatness of the whole. It is in free verse, but the shape is organic, not superimposed.

But poor as a beggar did I watch these two competitors,
My Caesar and Pompey of these later shadows.
Think now,
If the cards of fate had pawned in other fields,
Had they mantled in dead shade the glittering hero of that
    triumph
How the trumpets could transmute his African, lone death
To dancing maidens, cymbals, bending airs of music,
To wind in high cornfields of the Nile's black land
When they grow their golden hair above the green falling
    flood
And wind runs shaking out their purses of young seed,

  .   .   .   .

The spoils of Africa,
Sand from green rivers sieved and fired for gold

Must load his horns of plenty;
It will lie like honey but far heavier,
For sand, bitter sand, and never honey fills the hour-glass
Dropping in rhythm to the hours of honeyed light
That are matched in their cells of sun with this falling sad
    grain of sea ;
Skins striped with sunfire,
And monkeys, comic mirrors of our own bald shapes,
Are borne at the chariot wheel
With black prisoners, dead coals of hate.

Pompey is an arrogant high hollow fateful rider
In noisy triumph to the trumpet's mouth
Doomed to a clown's death, laughing into old age,
Never pricked by Brutus in the statue's shade.
But Caesar and Pompey were dead pawns to me
Moving down fields for ever fallow, never bearing,
And I cared not which killed the other
Snatching his mock-life of me;
While Donne and Gargantua, each in his sphere,
Walks without me and has the populace to work upon.
Each can win, each can lose, each can break his paper
    life,
Tugging at that kite through the thick and fiery winds,
Foul breath of crowds, battle pantings, whispered words
    of fate,
Till the string break,
When their souls survive but must forage for themselves,
For I cannot care for something that can never die.

But the whole of my speech to-night is a plea that
we should leave the known and the safe, and find
another land; and the only way to do this is for poetry
to be written by poets. The poetry of to-day has been
much debased by the sub-Wordsworthian ideals of
those versifiers who wrote verse which was fashionable

from 1900 till about five years ago, and who are, indeed, still read in certain quarters. To these men,
rhetoric and formalism were abhorrent, partly, no
doubt, because to manage either quality in verse the
writer must be a poet. But also, in the verse of that time,
as in much of this, the praise of worthy home-life
alternated with swollen inflated boomings and roarings
about the Soul of Man. These reigned triumphant,
together with healthy, manly, but rather raucous shouts
for beer, and advertisements of certain rustic parts of
England, to the accompaniment of a general clumsy
clod-hopping with hob-nailed boots. Yet, in spite of
this, the business man's careful logic was never absent,
combined, strangely enough, with the innocence of the
country clergyman (this last trait is dedicated to the
unfortunate Wordsworths). Those stronger members of
the populace who enjoy adventure could be taken for
rides in Walt Whitman's powerful steam-roller, crushing
even the stoniest roads. Then there was Mr. Lawrence's
hairy, or Jaeger, school of verse. Many things were
discovered; the only thing which was not discovered
was poetry. At the same time a school of Americo-
Greek posturants, resembling not so much marble
statues as a white-tiled bathroom, began to exude a thin
stream of carefully chosen watery words. Added to
these misfortunes, we are now afflicted by the shrill
moronic cacklings of the Sun-Realists, laying never so
much as even an addled egg, and by the erotic con-
fidences of rich young ladies, suffering less from an
excess of soul than from an excess of distilled spirits.
Again, a large section of the public mind that has not
been wilted away by this is still overshadowed by the
Aberdeen granite tombs and monuments, the classical

scholars of Victorian times, and by Matthew Arnold with his chilblained mittened musings.

The one thing to remember is this. Poetry is a strange flower which will not bloom in every soil. It is not the result of reason nor of intellect. It is the flower of magic, not of logic.

TRADITION IN DRAMA

By ASHLEY DUKES

IN common no doubt with others who take part in this series of addresses, I have begun by asking myself what is meant by tradition. Experiment we know: our lives are very largely governed by it, and we are able to see its practical results all around us. Thanks to experiment in thought and applied science, the pulse of civilization has been astonishingly quickened within our own lifetime. For that matter, much of modern literature is certainly due to experiment, and we are able to judge for ourselves of its adventurous course. But what is this tradition which forms the other half of the subject of our inquiry? Is it something upon which men agree, or upon which they differ? Is it a tangible reality, as far as anything can be a reality in the world of art, or is it a rather pompous shadow that overhangs the mind and threatens the independence of the living artist?

Consulting the dictionary, we learn that tradition is the handing down of opinions, doctrines, or practices from forefathers to descendants by word of mouth, without written memorials—a sufficiently formidable definition which does not lessen the anxieties of a speaker on the traditional side. For tradition in this sense represents impersonal authority, even arbitrary authority, since it rests upon tastes about which there is no disputing. It is idle to pretend that such authority is ever popular. Its supporters are necessarily on the defensive. They are liable to be abused in every generation as old fogeys, lifeless academicians, bigots, hierarchs, and despots. Every artistic urchin, so to say, will pull a long nose at them. These are the drawbacks of all authority, and especially of an authority that is not even written down in critical Bibles upon which men can agree to base their faith, but transmitted in word and practice from ancestors to posterity.

Yet properly considered, tradition is surely no more than the fruit of successful experiment. To my mind this definition is necessary because it establishes the idea of one single tradition in every branch of art— a tradition sufficiently broad to include the most diverse kinds of experiment, but at the same time sufficiently narrow to exclude the manifold failures and heresies with which the course of every human activity is encumbered. Let us dispose at the outset of the notion that there are several different and conflicting traditions in each form of art or literature—call them classical or romantic or realist or impressionist or what you will. There is only one tradition, to which each of these movements properly belongs, and we constantly see the best work of each movement separated by taste and experience from the inferior work and added to the main body of traditional achievement.

Thus within our own generation we have seen impressionist painters take rank among the great masters, and realist novelists and playwrights take rank among classical writers: and as far as anything can humanly be known, we know that this judgement we have formed of their merits will not be disturbed by the verdict of posterity. We are ourselves creators of this thing called tradition. It is not imposed upon us by the dead hand of the past, nor should it fetter the mind of the adventurous artist. If we are able to look upon tradition as successful experiment, it becomes a living element in our critical and creative work—living because it is ever changing and growing, and because its change and growth are our own.

Our subject on this occasion is tradition in drama, by which is meant the relation of the modern theatre, not only to the practice of the past, but also to this authority that is continually being renewed and re-created in the present. I speak of the modern theatre, and not of modern dramatic literature, because to me the theatre is a whole of which the written drama is only a part, and its tradition must also be regarded as a whole. The art of the theatre being of this composite character, I suggest that we discuss the theme of dramatic tradition under, say, three main headings. These are Tradition and Dramatic Literature, or play-writing: Tradition and Dramatic Performance, or play-acting: and Tradition and Theatrical Presentation, or that art of the theatre which seeks to establish harmony between the component crafts. And I think it will be found that these various traditions of writing, acting, and presentation continually depend upon each other, having grown and developed under each others' influence in centuries of achievement. Therefore I cannot promise a wholly literary approach to the subject. The tradition we have to examine will not show us the theatre as an appendage or echo of literature, but as an independent means of expression.

Tradition and Dramatic Literature. We must beware of confusing tradition with historical fact: but it will be necessary to recall something of the earliest dramatic history, if we are to understand the continuity of the traditional shape of drama. This continuity is in itself

very marked. When we compare a good modern play
with one of the great classical tragedies—say *The Wild
Duck* of Ibsen with the *Oedipus Tyrannus* of Sophocles—
we see that the resemblances between them are far
more striking than their differences. The introduction
and development of the theme, the movement to the
climax, the reaction and the catastrophe are almost
identical in essential conception and sequence, however
unlike the narratives may be. Were a citizen of old
Athens to be translated suddenly into the midst of our
present civilization, it is likely that our theatre, with all
its shortcomings, would be the only modern institution
really intelligible to his mind. The form of the playhouse, its curtain and its scenery would much astonish
him: but the movement of the spectacle would still be
familiar. In no other art, perhaps, unless it be in sculpture, are the productions of ancient and modern so
similar in their technical craftmanship and form of presentation. Sometimes we feel that nothing essential has
changed in the world of the theatre in the course of two
thousand years and more. Probably nothing essential
will change in the course of two thousand years to come.
It is certain that the drama may pride itself not only
on its antiquity, but on the perseverance of a form that
embodies classical conceptions even in the most modern
shape and subject-matter.

Having said so much of its continuity of form, let us
recall that drama originated as a branch of poetry.
Poetic expression is generally divided into three varieties:
the lyric, the epic, and the dramatic—that is to say, the
poetry of song, of narrative, and of action. The Greek
chorus first of all declaimed the poetry of action in the
human spirit. From that dramatic poetry there emerged

the dramatic impersonations of the chorus leader, and afterwards the dialogue of the poetic drama. It is doubtless the element of song that preserves the form of drama, and lies implicit in its rhythmic movement.

The traditional expression of poetry is metrical, and for centuries the dramatic dialogue of all plays, even of comedies and farces of contemporary life, retained the metrical shape dictated by the original inspiration of drama. The playwright was considered as a poet first of all, and his especial branch of poetry ranked with the highest. The Elizabethan dramatists, as we know, never forgot that they were poets. It was not until the later eighteenth century, when the greater number of plays were already written in prose, that the English dramatist surrendered this proud title and became a plain writer for the stage. For a hundred years and more, as many literary historians have noted, the English theatre became a negligible quantity in the world of letters: but this was precisely because the poets had ceased to write for it, or the persons writing for it had ceased to be poets. In other countries of Europe, where the nineteenth century was not so barren of dramatic poetry, the classical alliance of poetry and drama endures to this day.

Yet we open a London newspaper to find a literary critic asking, with reference to the classification of subjects in library or publishers' catalogues: 'What possible connexion can there be between Poetry and Drama?' To answer such a question, there is no need to go back to the time of the Greeks: it is enough to remember that the world's greatest poets are also its greatest dramatists. Literary criticism, one would suppose, could hardly overlook such a coincidence. There may be little apparently in common between poetry and the current productions of the stage: but that is surely the fault of the theatre, the playwright, and the art of presentation. We may note in passing that the revival of interest enjoyed by the English drama in the last two generations is chiefly intellectual, social, and critical: it is not yet a revival based upon a re-birth of the inspired and spoken word. Such a revival, when it comes, may not be literary in the accepted sense: it may even take an original theatrical form which repels the bookish mind: but it will certainly be poetic in spirit. Meanwhile the kinship between drama and poetry is plain enough. Both of them existed as manifestations of the living word before the days of literature began, and both of them will continue to exist as manifestations of the living word after the days of the cinema are ended.

Admitting, then, that the first tradition of drama is its rank as a branch of poetry, let us consider the special approach of the writer to his subject which constitutes dramatic authorship. Perhaps the sensible question to ask of him first is why he writes for the stage at all. What is his creative purpose? From the traditional point of view, this question answers itself in the simple assertion that the writer is a dramatic poet. He needs no other justification in writing for the stage, nor does he seek for any. Clearly this would have been the answer of Sophocles, of Shakespeare, and of Goethe to any inquiry regarding their purpose in writing plays. As dramatists they sought to move their spectators' minds; as poets to inspire their listeners. These are the traditional purposes of dramatic poetry. A dramatist with any other dominant purpose—for example, instruction, propaganda, criticism of generally received opinion, moral conviction, illustration of a thesis, whatever it may be—must necessarily break with the traditional school. He may be an adroit playwright, he may be an eloquent and witty preacher, he may do a vast amount of good in the world, he may be gloriously right where all the rest of humanity is ignominiously wrong; but he is not a dramatic poet any longer, and it is only by force of paradox that he can claim the title. Whatever be the merits of this break with tradition, let us recognize that it exists. The use of the stage as a personal platform is opposed to all conceptions of poetics that have been handed down to us. It may be that the intellectual drama of the late nineteenth and early twentieth centuries will itself bring some permanent contribution to the dramatic tradition. It may be also that the reaction from this same intellectual drama will direct writers' minds afresh into the simple channel of drama as an art form, and thus lead to a revival of dramatic poetry.

Once the question of purpose is disposed of, we may pass on to the dramatist's actual task, as it appears in the light of tradition. Having found a suitable subject, he proposes to tell a dramatic tale to his listeners. It may be the same tale that has been told a score of times by the epic poet; but there will be an altogether different manner in the telling, and the outward action, however swift and animated, will serve chiefly to illustrate the spiritual state and sensibility of the participants in the drama. The dramatist intends to interest us, not in events and characters alone, but in his special interpretation of them. This interpretation, according to the classical tradition, may assume one of two conventional forms. It may be either tragic or comic. In

contemplating a tragedy, where the characters are subjected to the repeated blows of Fate, the spectator will
be moved by pity and terror; whilst in seeing and enjoy-
ing a comedy, where familiar vices are scourged and
familiar follies ridiculed, his mind equally will be purged
by laughter and confirmed in wisdom and sanity.

It is now the fashion to assert that these divisions of
drama are out-of-date, and can safely be ignored by
the dramatist. It is true that our tragedies are few and
far between, and many of our comedies lack the ultimate
gravity of purpose that should be the justification of
their laughter. But we should hesitate before con-
demning tragedy or comedy on that account. The
division of serious drama into these two forms endured
for many centuries, and it is worth remarking that the
division of actors into tragedians or comedians lasted as
long. It is only within quite recent years that nondescript drama and nondescript acting have held the
stage. The masks of tragedy and comedy are the
cherished emblems of the actor's art, and it may very
well be that these masks of poetic form, symbolizing
the grave and gay moods of human nature, possess a
significance for the dramatist far deeper and more
lasting than that of literary conventions. Generally
speaking, we may say that a good play is the better for
being also a good tragedy or a good comedy, the
preservation of the mood and style imposing a most
helpful discipline upon the playwright's creative impulse. We may note also that writers of romances and
novels have not hesitated to borrow from the older
dramatic tradition in this respect, so that they also
preserve the conceptions of the tragic and the comic in
the treatment of a theme.

Assuming then that the dramatic poet proposes to write either a tragedy or a comedy, his next encounter with tradition will concern the dramatic unities, called the unities of place, time, and action. It is true that these unities were decreed by a dramatic critic named Aristotle, and playwrights may therefore pardonably look upon them with suspicion; but they have justified themselves so thoroughly in the course of dramatic history that their origin may perhaps be overlooked. Actually these famous unities amount to little more than deductions from the example of good plays. When a modern playwright determines to write a piece in which the scene shall remain the same throughout the action, the characters shall not be more than six or eight, and the events shall occur on one day, he is generally aware that this economy offers the best hope of getting his play performed; but, historically speaking, he is following the precepts of Aristotle and the footsteps of Sophocles and Aeschylus. After the time of the Greeks it was no longer insisted that the dramatic scene should remain unchanged during the course of a play, or that the events should occur within an arbitrary space of twenty-four hours; but the unity of action, decreeing the subordination of all incidents and dialogue to the main theme of a play, is in effect one of the definitions of drama itself, and the chief distinction between a tale as told on the stage and a tale as told in any other form of writing.

These are the essential and permanent traditions of dramatic composition. All the other conventions of the playwright's craft, and they are many, relate to forms and fashions which are subject to frequent change. Some of these forms are imposed by the physical limitations of the playhouse, others by the exigencies of the stage and the scenery, others again by the habits and customs of the audience.

How far does tradition govern the mind of the present-day dramatist? What does it actually mean to him? Is he aware of the antiquity of the art he practises; does he consciously profit by the experience of a hundred generations of fellow writers for the stage? These are difficult questions to answer, for the virtue of tradition lies in its unwritten nature. Such influences may be felt without being analysed or described. Good plays, observing all the unities, are daily composed by writers who have never heard of Aristotle; and as many bad plays are composed by critics whose task it has been for years or decades to form dramatic taste. The practical use of tradition may easily be overestimated; but dramatic history seems to tell us that from time to time a spiritual awareness of its own purpose arouses the theatre, as it were, from some period of indifference and lethargy, and in this awakening dramatic poetry is reborn.

Tradition and Dramatic Performance. Play-acting began in the performance of a religious rite at a popular festival. It grew into a form of recitation aided by the wearing of masks, costumes, high shoes destined to increase the stature of tragic personages, and similar embellishments; and by the use of elaborate and vivid gesture. The religious character of acting endured in some measure throughout the Athenian civilization; but under the Romans the players shed most of their morals with their masks and became a despised section of the community, mostly recruited from freedmen or slaves. The appearance of women on the stage did nothing to raise the character of public entertainment or the standing of the actor's profession. In the Middle Ages companies of actors wandered through the fairs of Europe, setting up their booths here and there to give religious mysteries, pantomimes, buffooneries, moralities, or masques. Princes and rich noblemen attached companies of actors to their households, and at the same time offered patronage to the poets who wrote their plays for them. The revival of drama in the fifteenth and sixteenth centuries, which was part of the general revival of art and learning, greatly improved the actor's position in the world; and it was about this time that he (or she) emerged from personal obscurity or local estimation to enjoy what in some cases was a world-wide fame. In the seventeenth century, when the great French dramatists were at work, the theatre was still principally an amusement of the world of fashion, and actors attached themselves eagerly to Courts like that of Louis Quatorze. The great English players of the eighteenth and nineteenth centuries did much to establish the actor's art on a more popular footing. To-day the actor is an acknowledged artist in a profession which has long ceased to bear the reproach either of vagabondage or servility.

Such in a few words is the outward history of acting, which often passes current for artistic tradition. To grasp the real evolution of the actor's art demands not only patient and scholarly research but a great deal of imagination, for the documents of dramatic performance are written only in the memory of the spectator. It is clear, however, that the technical craftsmanship of the actor has been conditioned as much by the requirements of the playhouse as by the demands of the dramatic poet. While he still wore the mask of Greek tragedy or comedy, his art found expression chiefly in gesture and dramatic presence. In the Elizabethan play-house, where he appeared unmasked but stood on a platform partly surrounded by spectators, he perforce cultivated elocution and rhetoric even more than the visual interpretation of his part. On the pictorial stage of the next generation of theatrical history, which is in all essentials the stage of our own day, separated from the audience by the proscenium arch, the actor was again obliged to develop the visual side of his talent. The tendency towards realism in his make-up and cos-tume was probably much accentuated by the increase of stage lighting. At the same time the more and more naturalistic methods of the playwright have deeply influenced the actor's technique.

When we speak to-day of tradition in acting, we mean a post-Garrick or post-eighteenth-century tradition. Whatever memory of earlier acting may have endured is now dissipated in the mists of time. The very names of contemporary Shakespearean actors are mostly un-known to us. We can only guess at the technical methods employed by the players of the medieval fairs. Some Roman actors are remembered for their wealth or other claims to notoriety. Of the Athenian players we know no more than of any other remote and anonymous priesthood. Yet however small the conscious part played by the past in influencing dramatic performance, tradi-tion means more to the actor than a superstitious un-willingness to speak the last line of a play at rehearsal, or a slavish insistence on performing the piece of Shakespearian 'business' that has been handed down from generation to generation without being entered in any prompt-book. The actor, like the playwright, began life as a dramatic poet. The verses he spoke were often his own; and were they another's, he was so far in sympathy with their burden that his personality was completely transfigured by the performance. There is a latent poetry of acting that appears from time to time in a modern play of our own experience, lifting the whole performance above the level of routine and commonplace; and in such moments of illumination we see before us the traditional actor, the classical actor, the inspired actor, who claims his right to the stage. It is certain that a revival of drama and theatre will always find the actor ready to bear his part as original artist and craftsman.

Tradition and Theatrical Presentation. If we make a round of the theatres of London at the present time, or for that matter of the theatres of Paris, Berlin, or New York, we shall discover that one form of theatrical presentation, which we may call the lifelike form, has been brought to the highest technical and artistic development. It is impossible to imagine any kind of play better 'done', to use the jargon of the theatre, than a modern play by Mr. Somerset Maugham, as presented in a good West End playhouse, with a cast of actors experienced in handling such work. The realism of the dramatist is expressed in a dialogue that is colloquial but at the same time forceful, supple, and sensitive. The realism of the actors nearly convinces us that the characters move on the same level of intelligence as the writer who portrays them. The realism of the setting makes an impression above all of quiet naturalness, of inevitability in relation to the subject and its conception. All is harmonious, all is distinguished. Only very foolish critics will speak of 'photography' in describing such a production. Dramatic realism was never photographic; it was always an art form, and it remains at its best a very interesting art form. It is even one of the traditional art forms, but it is not the only one, as a contemporary playgoer might be led to believe. Some of its masterpieces were already written thirty and forty years ago, and it is unlikely that any writer of to-day will improve upon them.

At the same time we should not suppose that this lifelike form of presentation is purely imitative or derivative. Mr. Maugham would probably have written good plays even if Ibsen and Strindberg and Tchekoff had never lived. The physical conditions of the playhouse and the advance of lighting and scenic construction would in any case have favoured naturalism in drama. The inclination of the actor towards a quiet and gentlemanlike or ladylike bearing has been growing for several generations past, and is not entirely unconnected with the advance of the profession in social prestige and standing. Moreover, the really photographic rivalry of the film was bound to exert a certain influence upon the theatre. All these reasons have contributed to make the lifelike play the characteristic and predominant form of presentation on our contemporary stage.

Traditionally speaking, it has the drawback that it is a dramatist's form, in the sense that it gives the dramatist power to dictate the whole of the theatrical process to his fellow craftsmen. To many minds this will appear a positive advantage. We have grown so accustomed to misquotations like 'the play's the thing', and to the assumption of authority by successive generations of playwrights, that a challenge to such authority seems at first sight perverse and even preposterous. For the dramatist's theatre is not only the theatre of ideas and argument, against which some artistic revolt might in the course of nature be expected; it is also the theatre of almost every practising playwright of the present day. The stage has come to be regarded, almost universally, as a vehicle for the translation of written into spoken drama.

But traditionally the theatre is something more than a vehicle of translation, however smooth and accurate. The theatre is an original language, just as poetry, sculpture, architecture, or painting are original languages. Traditionally the art of the theatre embraces drama, acting, play production, and the other theatrical crafts in one complete whole. This purpose of the theatre is stated in traditional practice, if not in traditional theory. The student of theatrical history can discover for himself that the periods most celebrated for their production of great drama have also been the periods of the most active theatrical collaboration.

At this point the student very reasonably asks 'And what becomes of dramatic literature?' Dramatic literature, to be frank, is the incubus of the stage. The theatre is connected with literature only to this extent, that some of its dramatic manuscripts are duly printed and circulated in book form. Having read them, the bookish or literary people naturally imagine the theatre to exist for the publication of drama, just as a printer exists for the publication of literature. They are confirmed in this judgement by finding that so many playwrights agree with them. Thus the theatre is delivered over bound to the conventions of another art, that of the written or printed word, and it continually suffers the reproach of not being sufficiently literary. The dramatic poet, of course, is claimed by literature as its own off-spring; but he is regarded rather as a prodigal son who wastes the substance of his Muse on riotous living among actors and actresses. Should he repent of such follies and return to the literary homestead, not only is the fatted calf duly killed for him, but his works are duly bound in its leather and placed respectfully upon the family shelf.

The student again asks very reasonably 'If the pro-duction of drama is not the purpose of the theatre, what is its purpose?' The answer of tradition is this, that theatre and drama together have but one purpose, the creation of theatrical art. No sensible person imagines that the theatre can do without the dramatist, even for a single evening. His is the brooding mind in which theatrical fancy first takes shape. His is the laborious and delightful task of writing and rewriting, moulding and remoulding this creature of his imagination during the months before the manuscript is entrusted to the theatre. Should he have bent his mind all this while to the sole purpose of theatrical art, then he has fulfilled his task as dramatic poet, and his work will already be fit for the stage in its general outlines, however many details need to be refashioned at rehearsal. Then he becomes the dramatist of tradition, and not the drama-tist of the dramatist's theatre, who is always preoccupied with the preservation of his literal text or the delivery of his intellectual message or some other extraneous matter that has nothing to do with the theatrical pro-cess. He must work for the theatre, instead of expecting the theatre to work for him.

Not that the dramatist should spend too much time in considering these fundamentals of his craft. In a healthy period of creative activity they will come as second nature to him. Shakespeare, we may be sure, never troubled himself with any abstract conceptions of theatrical art. He was too busily engaged in presenting himself at stage doors with a manuscript of his own or some one else's much rewritten, rehearsing actors in their parts with many additions to his text, trimming the whole production to suit the requirements of the playhouse, and looking for a good subject (seldom original) for his next piece. We know that such an approach to the theatre is not incompatible with the writing of the highest poetry. Are we not justified in calling it the traditional approach?

The student, persevering with his most reasonable questions, next inquires 'Would you be more precise in defining what you mean by theatrical art?' To my mind it is composed of four essential elements which I should call dramatic speech, dramatic acting, dramatic production, and dramatic scene. This implies a drastic change in the conventions of the current stage, where the realistic art form has been interpreted in terms of undramatic speech, acting, production, and scene, and their undramatic nature has been exalted into a positive virtue. We cannot ask that every writer for the stage shall be a great poet, but we can demand that every playwright shall speak the authentic language of the theatre in his dramatic dialogue. For that matter, we cannot ask of every actor that he shall be a genius, but we can demand of him some ability to transcend the commonplace of daily life. We should be unwise to hail as a great artist every one who can stage-manage a company and direct a performance; but we should be prepared to grant that good direction is as important to the theatre as good play-writing, and that the one is likely to inspire the other. We need not turn despairingly away from the dramatist and the actor to find the salvation of the theatre in the symbolism of the scene alone; but the theatrical appeal to the eye must be made through the work of an original artist. Above all, each of these must be a contribution to the whole, which is a work of theatrical art. We call them dramatic because drama denotes action and movement, and no other word can properly describe the quickening of the pulse of imagination and the heightening of effect which form the desired goal.

The traditional theatre is now threatened economically, if not artistically, by the upstart film. When we consider the positive advantages possessed by the theatre —the spoken word, the living actor, the graphic scene, the original creation of drama—we find that all of them are advantages more or less neglected by the realistic stage of daily experience, and capable of quickening and heightening only through a revival of theatrical presentation. The spectacular and sensational effects of the old theatre, such as horse-races and shipwrecks, are now much more effectively and expensively produced by the film. But there remain other encumbrances of the stage—empty and mechanical dialogue, passionate and dumb embraces, all the paraphernalia of pretended naturalism—which might well be removed to the studios of the cinema and turned into captions and close-ups. If we are to see dramatic photography at all, let us see the real thing as the film presents it and not the counterfeit as it is presented on the stage

by the small fry of playwrights who follow in the wake
of Ibsen, Shaw, and Tchekoff. From the moment when
the theatre realizes its real advantages over the film, and
resolves to use them, it will be threatened by no rivalry
at all.

This brings me to the subject of the film itself, which
may seem rather remote from our subject of dramatic
tradition. It is certainly a far cry from dramatic literature to the productions of Hollywood or Elstree. But
since we are speaking of drama itself, and not only of
the printed text, every form of expression should come
within our survey. The new art of the film, which is
the old theatrical art of miming treated in terms of
photography, offers some very interesting developments in presentation. There are no dramatists of the
film worth mentioning; or if there are dramatists, they
are only mentioned for the sake of form. I am told by
critics who take the film very seriously that it has now
reached a stage of development when it actually needs
imaginative writers. That is the film's own affair; but
hitherto the actors have been decidedly the most important artists in its making, and next to them rank the
producers or directors, who sometimes enjoy even
larger type on the posters. The film, in a word, has
understood how to make itself more theatrical than the
theatre, and that is one of its strong points. It deliberately composes its productions. It will never compete
with original dramatic performances, for photography
will always remain photography, whether the figures
walk or remain stationary, and the actual performance
can never be anything but a mechanical reproduction.
But the film, nevertheless, is undeniably a language, and
a dramatic language. The appearance of this new form

of silent speech reminds the theatre of its own purpose and its own destiny.

If we take a comprehensive view of the question, we see that the film itself is likely to be only a temporary phenomenon in dramatic history. Within a few years the progress of radio-telephonic invention will make it needless to go to a picture playhouse when we wish to see the mechanical reproduction of a play. The simple insertion of a plug at our own fireside will enable us to see some kind of dramatic performance projected upon the wall; and it may even be a very good performance, relaid from the best theatre available for the purpose. The ether, already congested by the other activities of the world's transmitting stations, may have to bear the further burden of the world's art and literature, made available by processes of science whose advance we now daily take for granted. If we then ask the film, not without malice, what becomes of its million reels of celluloid, the film may reply by asking us what becomes of our theatre with its curtain that goes up and down so and so many times in the course of the evening, and our actors who paint their faces to make them appear as though they were not painted, and our little bits of canvas scenery that look like our own parlours, and all the rest of the rather childish aids to allusion that are called theatrical. For that matter, what becomes of dramatic poetry?

These are hard questions to answer, but we may be sure of one thing. The theatre, which has endured a good many vicissitudes in the course of history, will not die altogether because the mechanically reproduced drama becomes radiophonic, stereoscopic, polychromatic, and indistinguishable from the real article. Nor will dramatic poetry retire altogether into the covers of books. There is one traditional element of dramatic performance and theatrical presentation which we have not yet taken into account, and that is the element of the assembled audience. Perhaps there is nothing that really distinguishes the theatre from the film or any future form of reproduced performance except this one essential thing—the creation of drama in the physical presence of the spectator. This it is that makes two successive performances of the same play, by the same cast, so strangely different; and this it is that makes playgoing such a pleasurable gamble. Every one knows how much the audience contributes to the mood of performance, and how much it has contributed since the first spring day when drama as we know it emerged from the chants of a chorus in some hollow of a Greek hill-side, and the players themselves became the audience.

As for the text of dramatic poetry, which is called dramatic literature, that too will endure in its traditional shape. For this text, although by no means the whole of drama, is as essential to the action of a play as words are essential to the action of our lives. And, moreover, this text is the indestructible part of theatrical art, the seed that can be put away on dusty shelves and neglected and even forgotten, and yet can come to flower again in the hands of new artists and before a new audience. So important is this text, preserving as it does not only the writer's original dialogue but all the changes made in it by theatrical experience, that we are justified in regarding it as the chief element in all dramatic creation. But if we think of this text alone as drama, we misunderstand the whole nature of the theatre.

On the right hand side of the road that leaves the modern town of Athens and winds up the hill to the Acropolis, within the railings of what looks like a public park, is the little theatre of Dionysos, where one may sit in the carved chair of the high priest immediately facing the stage, and imagine oneself a dramatic critic miraculously set free from the plush stalls of Shaftesbury Avenue and transported to this sunny place to think of theatre and drama. Behind the broken line of Graeco-Roman sculpture that makes the proscenium of the former stage there runs the broken line of hills and sea, just as it was seen as background by the spectators who assembled in the amphitheatre of benches surrounding the stage. In this place, on these very grave and sacred stones, were performed for the first time the tragedies of Sophocles and Aeschylus and Euripides; and of all the noble words that resounded in this theatre no more than the hundredth part is preserved to us in any written shape, the rest being fled into human forgetfulness as surely as sound itself, without some rock to give it echo, flees into distance and is lost.

But in reality it is not of drama alone that one thinks in the theatre of Dionysos; for on the hill above it rise the greatest monuments surviving to us from classical antiquity. They arc monuments of religion, of art, of social purpose; and we may justly and proudly reflect that the theatre ranks with them—that the city on this hill would have been incomplete without the stage on its slopes, that the community who dwelt here and gave us the tradition of every other art gave also the tradition of theatrical performance.

EXPERIMENT IN DRAMA

By C. K. MUNRO

I WANT to warn you to begin with that I am probably one of the most ignorant people in this room. I told your secretary that when he asked me to do this lecture, but he still persisted. I do not, therefore, stand before you as one who has studied modern drama more than you have. I have probably studied it less than most, and if, afterwards, any one asks me questions about obscure or even not obscure dramatists, the answer will probably be the simple one that I never heard of them. No, if I have any claim to stand here—and I very much doubt whether I have—it is not because I know more than any one else, but because my approach has perhaps been a little different. It has been the approach of one concerned to do—or to try to do—not of one concerned to know. While, therefore, it is purely personal, and may be of no general interest; and while it certainly lacks all scholarly method and completeness, it is possible that it may enable me to suggest a new point of view in some respects to you. If I can do that, it is all that I can hope and I shall be satisfied.

Well, I would not have brought in that explanation except that I think it is well we should know where we are, and also because what I am going to say is conditioned by it. I do not know whether it is usual for lecturers to tell you what they are going to do. I have a feeling that the creation and maintenance of suspense —a thing which I shall have something to say about in another connexion later on—is one of the weapons of a good lecturer. But as I am no lecturer, I propose to tell you straight off exactly what I am going to do.

First, then, I am going to consider what art in general and the drama in particular, is; a most unfashionable thing to do, and one which I believe it is usually considered the sign of an ignoramus to attempt. But unlike many people who talk about art, I find it difficult to get on without making some effort to define what I am talking about. Then I shall go on to consider in some detail the methods by which dramatists usually try to create something which will do the job of a dramatic work of art; and, finally, I shall hope to develop out of that a view of some of the efforts, and the meaning of them, that have been made by modern dramatists in the last twenty or perhaps fifty or sixty years.

To return then to my first question, what is a work of art? Well, I believe this can best be discovered by asking not what is, but what is *not* a work of art. What are the characteristics, that is, of experience which is non-aesthetic, of ordinary experience? And I will tell you why. Most people, it seems to me, fail to get any conception of what we may call, for want of a better term, aesthetic experience, because unconsciously they tend to regard ordinary experience as a complete, as a perfect mode of apprehension in itself. Now, you cannot add something to what is already complete. You cannot make perfect what is already perfect. So when people are told that art holds the mirror up to nature or expresses life, or shows you the world or any one of the hundred ways of saying this kind of thing, the instinctive feeling is—but what *more* is that than what I do every day? Now the answer is that you not only rarely do that, rarely see the world, see nature, life, and so on, but it is only at rare moments that you do anything remotely like it.

Ordinary experience, in fact, is not perfect, complete, from the point of view of observing the world. It is absolute make-shift and for the very good reason that this is not the object of it at all. It is not an end in itself, but merely a means to the end of surviving in the struggle for existence and seeing that those you are interested in survive. In this connexion, I should like to read you a passage from an essay by Mr. Roger Fry,[1] which is one of the few really penetrating things which I have come across on the subject:

'The needs of our actual life are so imperative that the sense of vision becomes highly specialized in their service. With an admirable economy we learn to see only so much as is needful for our purposes; but this is in fact very little, just enough to recognize and identify each object or person; that done, they go into an entry in our mental catalogue and are no more really seen. In actual life the normal person really only reads the labels as it were on the objects around him, and troubles no further.'

And again:

'We were given our eyes to see things, not to look at them. Life takes care that we learn the lesson thoroughly, so that at a very early age we have acquired a very considerable ignorance of visual appearances. We have learned the meaning-for-life of appearances so well that we understand them, as it were, in shorthand. The subtlest differences in appearance that have a utility value still continue to be appreciated, while large and important visual characters, provided they are useless for life, will pass unnoticed.'

There we have a statement of the poverty of ordinary

[1] Art.

experience as a method of really seeing the world from the special point of view of the plastic arts. But the same is true all round. We never see the world at all normally. We only see the tickets and labels which indicate *practical consequences* and so enable us to use what we see in our further negotiations in life, as a little consideration of the normal man's attitude to life will show. It is always considered that when one finishes doing one thing, one must at once begin *doing* another. Our children have hardly entered the world before we are training them to *do*—to walk, to talk, to learn. And they are thence projected into a career, the whole essence of which is doing: they have got to find a profession or business ('what is your boy going to *do*?'), to train for it, to practise it, to earn money by it, to get a wife, to bring up a family, to satisfy ambition, until the awkward moment when they're so old that they're only in the way. And how many continue this career of *doing* long past the time when there is any need for it, long past the time when they can be of any use—because the only meaning in life is got from doing, the only view of the world is as a place to be operated on. Ah, you will say, but this is the struggle for existence. We know we all have to struggle and work; but we also have our off-times, our holidays. . . . Unfortunately these only supply a still stronger proof of the only view we habitually take, because here we are free to express our preference. And how do we express it? Once more, by doing—by hitting balls about, climbing mountains, developing photographs, collecting something, and so on. Why, to many people the greatest condemnation of any holiday resort is expressed in the statement that 'there 's nothing to *do* there'. Mind! I am not saying it is wrong to do, or we can go without doing. I merely say that the attitude of doing things to the world and the attitude of contemplating the world are two totally distinct attitudes of mind, and the former is by far the predominant in ordinary individuals.

Now, so soon as we have got well into our minds that we normally never see the world at all, it becomes clear that if we could ever manage to do such an unusual thing as to see it, the result might be interesting, for it would represent a release from the eternal grind; the monster of struggle would be put to sleep, and we should find a *new way* of taking experience. To provide such a *new way* is the function of art.

This brings us to the question of how a work of art persuades us to this unusual activity. The answer is, by showing us a world that has meaning but no practical consequences for us, and making us attend to it. I want to repeat that. By showing us a world that has *meaning* but *no practical consequences* for us and *making us attend to it*. Now, the most obvious of the three elements in this statement is the second, that a work of art must have no practical consequences for us; and while not a sufficient, it is an absolutely necessary, condition of any artistic appreciation. There is a story of a sailor among the audience at a melodrama who, when the heroine on the stage exclaimed 'Will no one help me in my terrible plight'? called out: 'All right, Miss, I'm coming.' That sailor was not under the influence of aesthetic, but of what he took for real, experience. That heroine was not a thing to be contemplated by him. She was merely a thing bearing the ticket 'To be rescued'. Art, then, shows a world whose agitations never touch the world of actuality. But it must show us a world that has

meaning; that is to say, a world whose units have sufficient significance in terms of the real world to make
movement in the one interpretable in terms of the other.
This applies to the most abstract painting or musical
art. You cannot be interested in something that has
no meaning for you. It is the meaning that creates any
contact at all between the world of art and the audience.

But we have still one more condition. A landscape
has meaning, a single chord on the piano has meaning.
A photograph has meaning. We have now got our
audience to look, but we have not yet got them to
keep on looking. For this, interest must become
dynamic. It must not only be interest in what is
happening, but in what is going to happen. It is here,
in other words, that *form* enters in. The most obvious
function—not the only function, of course, but the only
one that I am concerned with here—of form in a work
of art is that it causes the work to present to the
spectator a continuous spectacle, which is not only
interesting at any moment, but suggests that something
of equal or greater interest is to come, and manages to
fulfil this expectation even down to the point of not
outraging it when what is to come is nil, that is to say,
at the end. When one considers that the spectator cannot be regarded as remaining throughout a fixed
quantity and therefore that his requirements are continually changing, it is at once clear that this matter of
form is somewhat complicated.

Well, now, we have our work of art with no practical
consequences, with meaning, and interesting enough to
make us keep watching it—is that all that is required?
On the contrary—it is nothing yet: we have got a

machine, it is true, which will persuade the spectator to do his bit; but we have not done ours until we have shown him something that is worth looking at. And that brings us right up against the question—what is worth looking at? We have said that so soon as you begin really to observe the world, you find it well worth doing—why is this?

Briefly and crudely the answer is that the spectacle which certain aspects of the world present to us has, if we put ourselves dispassionately under its influence, the power to widen the scope of consciousness by producing reverberations in the realm of the imagination; it becomes iridescent with the light that comes from all quarters of our experience, so that a single chord struck, a single impression produced in the foreground of the mind, immediately dissipates its energy backwards and becomes reflected in an ever-spreading wave that agitates every atom of our past experience, whether conscious or forgotten, that has any association with it; and by the pattern of these agitations, man is enabled to feel the universe in which he exists, to get in closer touch with the immensity of it than by any other means. Hence the importance of the process.

Well, that brings me to the end of my general remarks about art, but before passing on I should like to spend a moment or two on an inquiry which will become of some significance at a later stage. That inquiry is this: can we distinguish any types of experience in ordinary life that force a contemplative attitude upon us, and hence force us into receiving an aesthetic as opposed to a practical impression? I think we can, and a reference to them at this point may lend substance to the somewhat vague and transcendental descriptions into which

I have just been betrayed. Now following our rule, we should look for such types of experience in connexion with elements in the world that are elsewhere, either in time or place. The events of twenty years ago, or happenings at a distance, are less likely to have direct practical consequences for us than the events of here and now. And if we examine our impression of twenty years ago, if we think, for instance, of our youth, or of our childhood and compare it with our impression of to-day, I think we shall find just exactly the difference that, whereas to-day is weighed down with the apprehension of practical consequences and difficulties and is definite with a mass of trivial but distinct impressions, twenty years ago leaves no trivial impressions at all— possibly even no definite impressions—and is without any associated apprehension as to practical consequences; and hence possesses an iridescence, a significance, which is quite alien to our impression of to-day. In other words, we can see our life as a whole twenty years ago in a way which is impossible to us with regard to our life to-day. There may not be one single event or action which we can remember and yet we shall not for that reason get a poorer, but rather a richer, impression of the whole. The same is true of other places: to the man who lives in London, London is a place of practical consequences and possesses few romantic associations; what happens in London affects him to the exclusion of his ever observing it for its own sake. But promise him a trip to Paris and his imagination will become alive with anticipations of wonder; yet the inhabitants of Paris are strangers to this wonder and see in it as drab a place as the Londoner sees in London.

Perhaps, however, the most striking examples in which ordinary life produces these effects is when it brings us up against sudden and irrevocable changes. Let our companion of to-day die to-morrow and we shall suddenly gain an impression of him which we never had when he was alive; hitherto he has always been the man we saw an hour ago or are going to see this evening or who may do something we don't like; he has practical consequences for us. But, of a sudden, all that is swept away and in place of it we find ourselves suddenly face to face with the fact of life without him as compared to life with him and, through this, he is suddenly presented to us in one all-comprehensive impression of his whole significance for us.

Well, now, I am afraid that much that I have said in a general way about Art and Works of Art will have been familiar to most of you and perhaps I should not have wasted time on it; my excuse must be that in what follows I propose to relate the various developments in the drama which we shall consider to the fundamental processes common to all art, and this might have been difficult had these processes not been stated in some form or another.

And so, let us turn to the drama and dramatist. Here is a dramatist sitting down to compose a drama— what is the first thing he has to do? Well, first, as we saw, he has to create a world, a world that shall have *meaning* for his audience; and when we come to examine the thing in the concrete, we find that the dramatist's problem is not to avoid *no* understanding by his audience, but *wrong* understanding. In other words, we run here against the problem created by prejudice. Prejudice, not in its ordinary sense of prejudice *against*, but just prejudice in the sense of pre-judging, of judging beforehand. This is a question of tremendous account in the theatre and in my view one that is not usually given nearly enough importance. You may think you go to the theatre unprejudiced. You do not. You go packed with pre-belief as to what kind of thing you are going to see.

A simple example, which will sufficiently illustrate what I mean, is your attitude when you go to see a celebrated comedian whom you have never seen before. You will try to laugh at him all you can, and if he amuses you sufficiently to make this reasonably easy, you will be persuaded he is very funny and his reputation is deserved. In that case his reputation has helped him. But suppose, no matter how you try, you *can't* laugh; you will find that presently, unable to take any pleasure in his goodness, you will turn right over, decide he is a complete fraud, and snatch an unholy joy in discovering how bad he is. In this case his reputation has been partly his undoing. I have seen audiences in a theatre laughing unroariously at passages in a play that were not the least funny or intended to be, because they thought they *must* be funny, having been written by so and so—till they discovered they weren't funny, and then they decided so and so had failed. Such is the effect of prejudice, and, as I say, it is of vast importance. I believe that one of the greatest obstacles to the successful production of serious drama in the West end of London at the present time, is the fact that the most paying part of the West-end public does not *expect* to find in the theatre anything to think about seriously. It is not, you will observe, that they would not be willing

K

to do so if it could be conveyed to them that it was a thing worth doing, it is simply that their whole *prejudice* about the theatre is that it is a place to go to be amused and nothing else.

Now, what bearing has this on the dramatist? This: that the wise dramatist knows the vague half-enmitous, prejudiced eyes with which the average audience surveys the stage at the rise of the curtain, and will walk right in and seize it by the throat and say: 'Now, *this* is the kind of thing you are going to see.' The greatest enemy of success is puzzlement, and an audience with a new play will feel puzzled if it possibly can. It loves the attitude 'Well, I really cannot make out what it is all about'. You have only got to read the critics to see how they delight in saying: 'I suppose So and So meant something, but all I can say is I could not understand, &c.'

Now, in the old days, this was understood, and a means was found of getting round it, and that means was the stock-character. People nowadays talk of the old stock-character as a crude invention. It was nothing of the sort. It was an invention in line with the soundest canon that the audience must have co-ordinates of reference. It must know what instruments it is going to hear, or it will be thinking about them and not prepared with an open mind to listen to the tune. It is this prejudice, of course, that gives inertia to the evolution of the drama, to the evolution, indeed, of all art, for you cannot suddenly jump, because no one will be prepared for you or appreciate you.

Now, here we run, for the first time in this lecture, against something germane to what it is really supposed to be about, because one of the most striking features of modern experiments in drama has been the introduction, in spite of this prejudice, of all kinds of worlds and types of characters. If we consider that, even in England, we have had in the last thirty or forty years thrust under our noses the worlds of Ibsen, Strindberg, Wilde, Hauptmann, Maeterlinck, d'Annunzio, O'Neill, Tchekoff, Pirandello, Toller, to make a by no means exhaustive list—it will be clear what I mean.

At first the movement took shape in an extreme realism—a realism that has dominated the stage right down to the present day. The dramatist presumably felt that the safest way to abandon the stock type was to substitute the human type, which he presumed his prototype on the other side of the footlights would easily recognize and understand. But more recently, another and opposite means has been adopted, namely, the 'expressionistic'—I say more recently, though as a matter of fact there are elements of it to be found in certain plays of that curious dramatist Strindberg. This is really from this point of view not a further development, but a retrogression. The expressionist gets round the *prejudice*, just as the early writers got round the *ignorance*, of the audience by making his aim so obvious, and subordinating everything else to this end, that no one can miss it. You probably know or have heard of a play called *The Adding Machine*. I propose to read a short passage from that play to indicate what I mean when I say that the expressionist subordinates everything to making his aim so plain that no one can miss it. In this case his aim is to indicate that a certain number of people are mere ciphers in civilization, the common drudges who have no individuality, or if they ever had any have had it long ago suppressed. This is how the expressionist

does it. Here is the stage direction at the entry of these
individuals:

'Zero goes to the entrance door and opens it. Six men and
six women file into the room in a double column. The men
are all shapes and sizes, but their dress is identical with that
of Zero in every detail. . . . The women are all dressed alike
too. . . . The files now separate, each man taking a chair
from the right wall and each woman one from the left wall.
Each sex forms a circle with the chairs very close together.'

The scene, by the way, is an evening party given in
New York, by Mr. and Mrs. Zero to their friends the
Ones, Twos, Threes, Fours, Fives, and Sixes. Here is
a specimen of the conversation:

Mrs. Six. My aunt has gall stones.
Mrs. Five. My husband has bunions.
Mrs. Four. My sister expects in a month.
Mrs. Three. My cousin's husband has erysipelas.
Mrs. Two. My niece has St. Vitus's Dance.
Mrs. One. My boy has fits.
Mrs. Zero. I never felt better in my life. Knock wood!

The men have a similar conversation about agitators,
foreigners, &c., at the end of which is the following:

All (in unison). That's it! Damn foreigners! Damn
    dagoes! Damn Catholics! Damn sheenies! Damn
    niggers! Jail 'em! Shoot 'em! Hang 'em! Lynch
    'em! Burn 'em! (They all rise.)
All (singing in unison). My country, 'tis of thee,
    Sweet land of liberty. . . .

Now that, I think, will sufficiently indicate what I
mean when I say that the expressionist subordinates
everything to making his purpose so clear that no one
can miss it. . . . Mr. O'Neill has recently produced in

a play called *Strange Interlude* what seems to be a curious combination of realism and direct expressionism in this sense. The general basis is realistic, but the characters speak thoughts which flash through their minds—this being indicated by the complete immobility of every one meanwhile. This play has been a success in New York, which suggests that the arrangement is effective. On the other hand, I am told a great deal of the effect is got through the comic incongruity of the thoughts with action and speech. If this is so, while the device produces what is quite legitimate comedy, there is nothing particularly new about it, from a dramatic point of view.

But I see I must utter a warning here. Do not think that what I am saying has in practice much to do with the environment in which the action takes place. You can have stock-characters in hell, earth, or heaven, sea or land, and dressed as yokels, or animals, or anything you like. The ghost in fact was one of the stock-characters. You can have expressionism in a suburban dining-room and realism in the next world, and the play from which I have just quoted supplies, as a matter of fact, an amusing example of that. At the beginning, while the hero is on earth, the technique is of the most advanced non-realist type. Then he gets electrocuted for murdering his employer, and thereafter wanders about the most unlikely quarters of the universe, weird twilit worlds of the dead or the unborn—in every one of which, however, everything happens according to the most traditional realism.

Well, so much for the first thing the dramatist has to do to get his world set, to seize his audience by the throat and throttle its prejudices as to what it was going

to see. The next problem that must occupy the dramatist—consciously or unconsciously—is still connected
with the world he is going to present, and is the problem
of distance. From what psychological distance is the
audience going to be shown this world? On the one
hand, they may be brought very close, so close to the
figures in the drama as to feel them intimately and feel
that they know them. The advantage of this is that such
an audience becomes extremely sensitive and a great
effect can be obtained with very small means. The
disadvantage is that such an audience will be extremely
sensitive to anything improbable in what happens, or
what is said, and the dramatist is, therefore, chained
down to a very tight naturalism. If he doesn't put his
world in such close proximity to his audience, on the
other hand, he cannot get such sensitiveness, but he has
more latitude in what his actors say or do. Now, one
of the most remarkable developments in modern drama
has been the diminution in this distance. It is, at any
rate so far as I know, historically true that dramatists
in the early stages of drama—drama as opposed to
ritual, that is to say—worked with the most terrific
and horrific materials so as to obtain the best effect;
but as is always the case—and this is an absolutely
fundamental psychological consideration—the audience
adjusts itself, and the more tremendous the deeds upon
the stage (unless enormous care is taken to keep the
audience close), the more the audience tends to alienate
itself, so that the means defeat the end. Tremendous
deeds are not usual, they are inherently improbable,
and this tends to put the audience at a distance by
making them feel that they are looking at something
which, while it may be very significant, has not any very

close connexion with themselves. Broadly speaking, it may be said that the most overwhelming moments of great drama, such as Shakespeare sometimes achieves, arise from a combination of closeness with tremendous-ness. Shakespeare, in particular, had a knack of putting an audience by a single sentence right close to some one at the moment of overwhelming calamity.

This is as regards tragedy, but the same is true of comedy. It must happen, I think, to most people who try to write comedy that at some point or other it occurs to them that so and so would be extraordinarily funny. What then is it that is stopping them from putting it in? The trouble will be discovered to be that it is of the wrong texture. It is probably too coarse. It has not that natural inevitability upon which the whole of the rest relies for effect: it would outrage the whole basis upon which all other effects have been built. Here, again, it is a matter of balance. You can be extremely funny, exaggeratedly ridiculous at the expense of pro-bability, and have your audience far off. That may not matter then, because the effects you are putting over are so strong that they will carry. Or you can have your audience so close that they will appreciate the slightest and most subtle humours.

Now, the main characteristic, as I say, of modern dramatists, at least until very recently, has been the development of the effects of small distance, which has inevitably, by the process I have explained, gone hand in hand with the development of realism. In almost every sphere of drama I think it true to say you will find, in considering this balance I have spoken of, the tendency to subdue events to conform to probability and intimacy. If you look on the theatre of to-day, or rather of yesterday, you will find not one play in which tremendous things happen for every ten in which we are gently amused or interested by mild things happening. And the most remarkable figures from this point of view, the acknowledged masters like Ibsen, have been people who can, without outraging this canon, pack more intense and tremendous things into their drama than other people. You will note, by the way, a rather interesting contrast here. Since Shakespeare's drama was a drama of greater distance, his triumph was not to put tremendous things on the stage effectively, but to diminish the distance while doing so. Ibsen's drama being a drama of smaller distance, his triumph is not to bring the audience close—they are there already—but to be able to put tremendous things on the stage, yet keep them there.

To return, however; from Lytton and Robertson downwards, we have the whole school of drawing-room drama, and on the other hand we have the theatre for the first time the scene of intimate psychological studies with slow developments and small action. Recently there has been a change. It has been heralded in the commercial theatre by the coming of the crook drama, full of thrills and murders and all kinds of horrific events, but much more important from the point of view of the drama in general, by expressionism or impressionism. Seen from this angle, expressionism means simply the complete abrogation of all those touches which dramatists have hitherto adopted to put an audience at some distance, at some nearness, to the characters in the drama. It is the drama of infinite distance. If you will look at most drama, you will see that the dramatist has tried in any scene to solve a problem among others which might be formulated as follows: 'How can I make this character come on and say dramatically but naturally what he has to say?' The expressionist writer simply brings him on without any thought of naturalism—the character may not even represent, let alone *be*, a human being—and makes him express, often not by words at all, the essence of what he has got to do. The gain here is clearly a gain in economy, but there are other gains which we shall consider later.

So much then for the focusing of the world which the dramatist presents. He has now got a world with meaning to it, and has decided on the proper distance from which the audience should look at it. His next problem is how to *keep* them looking. I believe that while there are many ways of intensifying interest and a desire to see what is going to happen, there is only one mode of *creating* it and that is through *suspense*. The quality of suspense alone will carry a whole entertainment without any other aid whatever, even though that entertainment may not produce any aesthetic impression. The best example of this that I can think of is the detective story or the crook drama.

Now the most interesting thing that has happened, it seems to me, in this connexion in recent times has been the rise of the so-called intellectual drama which followed Ibsen. Shaw has said a good deal about Ibsen and the discussion drama; and following Ibsen there has arisen a whole school, of which Mr. Shaw is a leading exponent, for exploiting this kind of drama. Now the fact is that Ibsen seems to have been the first to discover that an audience can be held in suspense not only over what is going to happen to people, but over what is going to happen to an idea. And the more important, profound, and suggestive the idea involved, the more intense the suspense. This is very important because it is here, it seems to me, that there has arisen a complete misapprehension with regard to Ibsen. He has been regarded as a preacher or teacher or reformer. The reason and the only reason why Ibsen chose social problems as he did is to be found not in society but in the theatre. He discovered that you can keep an audience seated *better* by posing before it a really profound and interesting problem than by a mere triviality, but he used this fact as an artist should, merely to create and hold suspense. The main effect of his work, its main purpose, lies not in this at all, but in the final task of the dramatist which we shall consider in a moment, the rousing of the imagination. But a misunderstanding of Ibsen seems to me to have affected many critics, so that one still finds critics who talk of the 'problem' in connexion with a play, and of its 'solution' as being satisfactory or the reverse exactly as if a play were an essay or the proof of a proposition. The truth is that the only function of a 'problem' in a play and its 'solution' is to *hold your attention*. If it does this successfully to the end the solution is aesthetically satisfactory, whatever it may be logically; and if it does not, it has failed, no matter how irreproachable from the logical standpoint.

Now, the introduction of the *idea* has had a profound effect upon the drama. For it has brought to bear, besides a profundity from an intellectual point of view, which was lacking before, a new weapon of interest— the argument. People often talk about this. They say: 'Is argument on the stage permissible?' Well, the answer is quite simple. If the argument is about generalities,

and its solution purely academic, most certainly not.
You may create a certain amount of suspense as to the
outcome of the argument, though if it is not germane to
the main interest of the play, it is difficult to see even how
you can do this; but you are bound, when your argument is over, to leave the audience in the air and make
a complete discontinuity in getting back to the drama in
hand. But if the next step—and particularly a highly
dramatic step in the drama—depends upon who wins the
argument, then an argument can be as exciting as a fight.

So much for suspense. We have now got our audience
to understand, to look at and to keep on looking at the
drama and to do so from the proper distance. Were I
making a more systematic survey of the tasks before the
dramatist, I should now have to refer to certain qualities
which I may call 'intensifiers of interest'. These are of
great importance. Indeed, many people in speaking
of the drama would give the impression that they are
the only things of importance. I shall pass them over,
however, because I cannot think of any distinctive contribution which modern writers have made with regard
to them; they appear in every drama in some form or
other, but not essentially differently in modern from
what they did in the older drama. That leaves us free
to get on to the final aim and object of it all—the
rousing of the imagination.

Now here again, were this a general survey, I should
have to make a rather long excursion in considering the
relation of *form* to this matter. Luckily, however, for
you—and also probably for me—I am saved this task,
owing to the fact that this relation is so profoundly
embedded at the base of all drama—at the base of all
art—that the developments of recent times have not

made any essential difference to it that I can see. There are, however, certain other factors that have been very much affected, and which we must therefore consider; and since this is the most elusive part of the subject, I feel it will be very difficult to speak about the process involved itself and propose to construct a crude model—that must not be taken too literally—which I shall use for the purpose of argument and illustration. This model is in the form of a piano or rather a spinet—because a thing with no resonance at all is better—and then behind it but not connected with it, a great set of organ pipes. We have been occupied so far with the piano and how to strike notes on it; notes struck on the piano correspond to impressions and ideas conveyed by a drama. We have now to consider the organ pipes in which reverberations are set up by notes struck on the piano, for the organ pipes correspond to the realm of the imagination.

Two points I would note first of all. To every note on the piano there is not a corresponding organ pipe—in fact, quite lively tunes can be played on the piano without much response from the pipes. Dramas can be quite lively and exciting without having much imaginative significance. Secondly, when an organ pipe is wakened up, its great reverberation is of such a power and splendour that nothing on the piano can possibly compete with it. Herein lies one of the most fascinating difficulties and complexities of all creative art. Force, power, energy, diligence, violence—none of these are any use in themselves if the wrong note is struck : a note that hasn't any organ pipes in resonant sympathy with it. You can bang as much as you like but you will only be banging the piano. But strike one of the right notes ever so lightly, and you will awaken reverberations in the pipes on a scale of power far beyond any the most violent banging on the piano could possibly achieve.

Well, now to come back to the consideration of the drama. The most obvious fact about our modern drama is that we have abandoned one of the main weapons used by older writers for producing reverberations in the imagination, namely, poetry. I am inclined to think (though I may be quite wrong) that this fact is not unconnected with the diminution of distance in the modern drama about which I spoke some time ago. The poetic drama is bound, I believe, usually—perhaps not always, but usually—to be a drama of considerable distance. We have diminished distance and with it we have ruled out the possibility of poetry. But we have developed instead two methods which I may classify as Symbolism and the Creation of Atmosphere, which I think are both closely connected with the small distance of the audience and demand, for their efficient working, the close co-operation of the spectator. In addition to this there is another quite different device recently attempted which I may call the direct non-intellectual presentation of Expressionism.

Now in seeking for the genesis of the two main alternatives which we have developed, we must, I believe, return to our old friend Ibsen, who was at any rate an early practitioner of both, and used the one—symbolism —over-ingeniously; and the other—the creation of atmosphere—marvellously.

Symbolism, I am inclined to think, is a bad weapon anyway; at any rate in its crude form it is a curious automatic device guaranteed to work, as it were, some-what in the manner as the devices of the metaphysical poets were guaranteed to work; it is, in fact, a formula. What you say is this—and you will excuse my now abandoning my model in favour of the reality because I think in this case it is easier—what you say is, I want to stir up waves in the imagination. Very well; I shall keep what I am really talking about well in the background, but I shall invent an obvious symbol for each element in the situation; then I will talk about the symbols, and by association waves can be guaranteed to travel back to the realities away behind and stir up the imagination as they go. It was in this manner that Ibsen invented his *Wild Duck* so that when you are talking about the wild duck and the shooting of it and its going down to the depths, and so on, you are really talking about old Ekdal, and probably about some other things as well, for, as I say, Ibsen was over-ingenious in this matter. (He seems, indeed, to have been proud of his capacity to weave one pattern in the front and one at the back, having an absolute one to one correspondence—proud to the extent of sometimes ruining his effects, for he will actually hold up his action and destroy a wonderful atmosphere created by less mechanical and more artistic means in order to round off and indicate to you the last perfections of the correspondence. 'And I heard harps in the air.' He actually kills that splendid phrase by going out of his way to let you know that he has even got a reality to correspond to those harps, namely, Solness praying on the top of his tower.) But in that better device—the creation of atmosphere— Ibsen was, I think, almost unique in his power of combining intense suspense with intense imaginative reverberation. Most dramatists when they have worked up to an intense emotional climax, tend to poise the action there while they exploit the atmosphere; Ibsen never pauses in this way; he can get his action going full speed while maintaining intense reverberatory effects. Indeed the last scene of *The Master Builder*, to which I have just referred, itself affords a fair example.

Turning now to what I have called 'the non-intellectual presentation of expressionism' I may say at once that I regard this as a method which has not yet proved its power in practice, and so I do not propose to spend very long on it. So far as I can see, the expressionist starts from the undoubted fact that art works by presentation, not by description; that is, that only presentation and never argument or discussion—*qua* argument and discussion—can produce reverberations in the organ pipes. The sight of a woman weeping may start the pipes, but the statement 'A woman is weeping' can only play the piano; true, if the woman is a particular woman with whom emotional associations have been built up, the statement may play notes that will start the pipes, but the statement itself will have no part in this effect. The expressionist, therefore, tries to *present* everything. There is a point—I think it is in Toller's drama *Massemench*—where some one, I forget who, is haranguing some one else, and Toller wants to produce reverberations by the use of the theme that the man speaking is really everyman and therefore, when he speaks to some one else, that some one else is himself. Now, we admit that the statement 'You are really me' has no reverberation. But we can imagine the poetic dramatist producing a profound effect on this theme; Shakespeare might have done it in *Hamlet*. What does Toller do? They are all in masks, and Toller suddenly makes the second figure assume, unseen, a mask identical with that of the first. Now, that is presentation; there it is, like a picture—you can take it or leave it, but anyhow he has avoided arguing about it or describing it. This method might be looked upon, indeed, as an endeavour to cut out the piano altogether.

Now, as I say, this method has theoretical warrant, but I am bound to say that the theoretical warrant does not seem to be understood by the expressionists themselves, for they appear to me often to use it, not to achieve direct presentation, not to try to cut out the piano, but to bang over some intellectual statement—in fact, to bang *on* the piano. The latest example I have come across of this is in *Hoppla*, in which after a certain situation there is thrown on a cinema screen the inquiry whether the world, as presented in the play, can be regarded as normal. It is easily seen that this, while it uses the shorthand methods of the expressionists, is the exact antithesis of presentation.

Well, now that I have more or less gone over the ground, I am appalled at the scrappy, inconsequent, inaccurate, and generally inadequate mess I have made of it. I cannot hope to remedy this, but I can perhaps fill up a few of the gaps if I devote, as I propose to do, my final few moments to what I regard as by far the most really revolutionary dramatist of the last few years —I refer to Anton Tchekoff. He is so peculiar that there is something special to notice about his work under every head that I have covered.

I said that Tchekoff is really the most revolutionary dramatist. Let me remind any one who may think this is an odd thing to say about his quiet plays that it is enormously important in the theatre to distinguish between real novelty—novelty of method—and mere exaggeration or banging or oddity. Any play can be made to look extraordinary if it is produced in a sufficiently extraordinary manner; any play does have a superficial air of novelty if the characters are sufficiently fantastic—animals or fairies or forces or what not, or if the scene is laid in some sufficiently fantastic quarter of the universe. But it is not in these things that real originality lies; to discover that you have to consider the dramatist's problems—some of which I have tried inadequately to indicate—and to ask whether there is really anything new in the solution. And if we do this, we find that the methods of solution adopted by some of the most superficially odd dramatists are along standard lines; but we shall find in the quiet Tchekoff novelties that are almost startling in nearly every department. And first, as to the matter of distance. Close as the audience had been getting to the stage world previously, Tchekoff, I think, can claim to have brought them so much closer as to produce an effect different in kind rather than degree. For Tchekoff, owing to this quality, can occupy the stage for minutes at a time with effects—significant perhaps—but so trivial that no other dramatist would attempt them.

Consider the following passage from *Ivanoff*:

Shabelski. Nicolas, my dear boy, do please take me with you. I might possibly be amused a little by the sight of all the fools and scoundrels I should see there. You know I haven't been off this place since Easter.

Ivanoff. Oh very well! Come along then! How tiresome you all are!

Shabelski. I may go? Oh, thank you. (Leading him aside.) *May I wear your straw hat?*

Ivanoff. You may, only hurry please.'

L

Any one but Tchekoff would never have thought to occupy the stage with the line about the straw hat except as a somewhat broad comic point, and then he would never have written the next one. In Tchekoff such things are not essentially comic, but simply human.

Next we come to the matter of suspense and here, of course, it is that Tchekoff's peculiarity is most celebrated. It is often said that nothing happens in his plays; there is no suspense. Now, this is simply not true, as any one will discover who goes to a play where the suspense is really inadequate, and then goes to a play by Tchekoff. What Tchekoff discovered about suspense is this: that you can be kept watching when nothing is happening provided at any moment you think something is going to happen. This is a common experience in life; you turn into a street and see a crowd lining the pavement—something is coming; some kind of a procession—the King, the Prince of Wales, or some one—you do not know what it is, but you will join the crowd none the less eagerly for that and, what is more, you will find that not one in ten are any wiser than you. Now that is what Tchekoff applied to the theatre; for a long time perhaps nothing very much happens, but all the time we have the feeling that something is going to happen, and may happen at any moment. And when we come to the next department— that of playing on the organ pipes—we realize what freedom Tchekoff has got in his efforts to do this by his discovery about suspense.

You may remember I said that Ibsen had a miraculous way of getting on with the drama while playing on the organ—in other words you can still hear his piano indicating how the tune is going, even when the organ reverberations are loudest. Tchekoff has solved the problem by being able to do without his piano at all for long periods through making you feel confident that he is going back to it sometime and may do so at any moment; and it is this that has given him the opportunity to become the great modern master creator of atmosphere. With his audience so close that they are sensitive to the slightest developments, with an air of suspense which is as good as real suspense, Tchekoff seems to me to be the only dramatist who has gone anywhere near providing by other means an opportunity to concentrate on playing the organ pipes, equal to that enjoyed by the old dramatic poets; and the outcome is what has been aptly called, 'his centrifugal effect'—an effect in which the attention of the spectator seems to be literally taken and thrown outwards from the scene witnessed to the universal patterns in life of which it is a symbol. There is an astounding moment in the second act of *The Cherry Orchard* where out of the most unpromising materials in the world, namely, boredom and futility—boredom and futility I mean, not as themes and so on, but portrayed before you on the stage—he builds up an intense dramatic tension, a tension so great that when he wants to break it he has to adopt the odd but remarkably effective device of the sound of a rope breaking in a mine, heard away across the plain. Possibly the best example, however, is the last half of the last act of *Uncle Vanya*. If you compare Tchekoff's atmospheric effects with those of any of the atmospheric school, you will see how superior they are; there is no false magic about them. And Tchekoff is equally, it seems to me, the great modern exponent of symbolism. There is one example of bad—of obviously logical—symbolism in Tchekoff: it is the 'Seagull' which is not only a seagull, but also representative of the heroine. Compare that to the symbolism of Uncle Vanya shooting at the professor and *missing*, and we see the difference between good symbolism and bad. There is in the last case no futile ingenious logical correspondence; the act is simply typical of the whole man and therefore the most natural thing in the world.

One final point of interest about Tchekoff: he was curiously aware, in his art, of the power of those moments in ordinary life which I have referred to as forcing us to contemplate life and so give us a quasi-aesthetic experience, which are usually connected with *other* places, *other* times, and great irrevocable change.

You will find use being made continually throughout his dramas of the iridescence of other places—Moscow, to which the Three Sisters were always going but never went; of other times—*The Cherry Orchard* is full of references to better times past, and *Uncle Vanya* to better times to come; and finally of irrevocable change: at least three of his last acts might be said to be taken up with nothing else.

TRADITION IN BIOGRAPHY

By A. J. A. SYMONS

THERE are more difficult, and there are easier, ways of writing than the biographical, but no other in which the English genius has shown itself so uncomfortable and constrained. The novel, the essay, the lyric, even the poetic and the epic-drama, have enjoyed, in England as elsewhere, a spasmodic Golden Age; yet each of these is an artificial form, requiring the observance of convention and rule. Biography alone has as its simple subject the life and acts of man, in all their majesty and meanness; biography alone has no convention save the sober one of truth; and yet biography alone has failed.

Quantity, alas, is not the measure of that failure. Thirty years ago Lang wrote:

> For now a dentist cannot die
> And leave his forceps as of old
> But o'er him, e'er his bones be cold
> Begins the vast biography.

and still no one, from cricketer to criminal, can escape the cold tomb or colder tome. But, if not in quantity, at least in quality, English biography has lamentably failed. It has failed in beauty as it has in truth: in beauty, for what biography could be re-read for the pleasure of its form alone? and in truth, for biography is still a form of panegyric. Its future is uncertainly hopeful; its past history is certainly bad; for so far as it has a tradition it has a *bad* tradition; and though of all forms of art it has perhaps most to say, it has certainly, in the way of accomplishment, least of all to show.

What it *has* to show, the shelves of every public library miserably reveal. There, in petrified and meaningless solemnity, stand the biographies of yesterday: long rows of *Lives and Times*, *Lives and Letters*, or unadorned but still intolerable *Lives*, testaments perhaps, to the affection of relatives or the industry of hacks, but not to the intelligence of the biographer. Constructed on the simple formula of chronological sequence, they begin, for the most part, with their subject's birth, and describe his curly-headed innocence, his sailor suit. Chapters two and three, which show no diminution of the one or discarding of the other, are headed 'Schooldays' and 'Alma Mater', and precede 'Early Manhood' in which a passing reference to 'wild oats' shows that the author also has experienced much; and then chapter five, 'Marriage', sets us on the trail for home. 'Life in London', 'Early Work', and 'Later Work' lead naturally to 'Last Days': a death-bed scene, several moral reflections, a list of the books or acts of the victim, and one more biography is on the shelf, probably to stay there. This is the briefer style. Larger works, in more volumes than one, require a different technique, and may be padded by the dull transcription of their subject's letters, or the dishonest copying of contemporary accounts of whatever place the hero happens to be at, mixed with reminders that 'Shelley was then nine years of age and Wordsworth twelve; George IV was King, Canning Prime Minister; and though ten years had passed since the battle of Waterloo, the Corn Law Repeal Act had not yet been framed'. The only possible comment on this elaborated method is that it requires almost as much patience to write as it does to read.

How far, indeed, biography has failed may be determined by a simple test. What well-read person, not a trained expert in the subject, could write down from memory the names of fifteen English biographies that are not only in the first rank of their kind, but possess positive value in themselves as literature? To name fifteen novels or poems satisfying this condition would be easy enough; or, if difficult, the difficulty would lie solely in the task of selecting from many excellences; but if we omit the works of Mr. Lytton Strachey and his followers, wherein the perceptive see the belated stirrings of a new spirit, which *are* our great biographies? Boswell, certainly; Lockhart's *Scott*, if you will; Cavendish on Wolsey deserves a place, and Walton's *Lives*, though over-subjective, must be included also. If the names of Aubrey, Anthony a Wood, and Froude are added to Macaulay's *Essays* and Johnson's *Lives of the Poets*, how much that is notable will be omitted? And even from this list how much gives us the pleasure of literature in addition to the knowledge of fact?

Astonished by this paucity of masterpieces, we may well ask ourselves if there is not something inherent in the nature of biography that precludes its practice as a form of art; but such a conclusion would be cowardly as well as false logic, for what has been well done once can be done well again, and the existence in any medium of a single masterpiece implies the possibility of more. If we analysed Plutarch and Boswell, or Izaak Walton and Cavendish, surely we could deduce, from the skeletons of their works, the principles of their art? We could; but the analysis would involve much historical research, and more expository space. What I shall attempt, in the brief time I am permitted, is to compare the tradition of biography, as exemplified in the practice of the past, with the attitude of the new biographer, as he may be conceived in the future, with the hope that from the comparison there will emerge a fresh and attainable alternative to the dry imbecility of the ordinary 'Life'.

Looking, then, in a general and undiverted way at the rubbish heap of these books, it is not difficult to see consistence, of a sort, in their endeavours. What that consistence is, I have somewhat slightingly shown; but it has, in its longer forms, more serious claims. The *intention* of these annotated lives, from the single volume of Symonds to the five-volume monument of Buckle, is it not to *record*, to record *completely* and impersonally, to write out all the evidence, to retain the memory of a great man in his every moment? Some such claim, surely, would be advanced by any intelligent defender of long biographies; and that very claim is the key to the whole fallacy of our biographical attitude. Completeness is not merely impossible; it is undesirable. If the law of society imposed no restrictions upon writers, the law of human boredom would take its place; it is probably as much because the suppressed parts of Pepys are dull, as because they are disgusting, that they remain suppressed. But even if our patience were inexhaustible, biographical 'completeness' would remain a mere figure of speech, attainable only by arranging for the dead man to relive his days; for no biography, even if it have as many volumes as the *Encyclopaedia Britannica*, can record more than selected moments in its hero's life.

It is upon this impossibility of completeness that I base my argument. I suggest that biography would not so long have wandered in the wilds if from the first its object had been, not to record, but to reveal. Revelation, as Miss Gertrude Stein might say, Revelation is Explanation. Since selection is forced upon us, is the limiting condition of our work, is it not clear that we should include only what is significant, and omit what is not? But how can we decide what is significant without in fact *editing*, without wilfully putting forward one aspect of the subject? That is, in a clear view, what happens; for the combat between the new biographical spirit and the old biographical tradition is not that of method; both *select*, one knowingly, the other unaware; the true battle is between the unguided instinct, and self-conscious technique; and I am on the side of self-consciousness. If, before biography were written, its writer were to remind himself that he has space only for certain of the facts, that every fact he admits must be a brush stroke in a preconceived picture (preconceived by the writer) and carry its due weight, like a stone in an arch, then we should have fewer of those gloomy manuals printed just in time to be remaindered. But remember; such selection implies another task. It is always more difficult to understand than to copy; and that, in effect, is what I suggest the biographer must do. He must understand; for how else can be explain? How can he make clear to others what is not clear to himself. And to understand such difficult and complex subjects as Bernadotte, Poe, Nelson, or Oscar Wilde, calls for high talents. The difficulties are many. If we write the truth of a dead man, it is scandal; of a live one, it is libel. The mere suspicion that you are likely to be indiscreet, as they call it, makes relatives of the distinguished dead secretive. And even when the facts have been established, they must be reconciled, and to reconcile the seeming contradictions of character, the reading of many books is not enough. The ideal biographer of the future will perforce know many things hidden from his past and present colleagues. From the standpoint of a mechanized age, he will look back over a dead, unmechanized space of time; and in that solution he will see the figures of his themes. Possessed, from the first, of exceptional insight into the oddities and moods of man, and dowered also with exceptional curiosity to bear him through the tiresome task of necessary research, he must claim at least a passing acquaintance with medical and neurological science. Neurological science; for he will write, not of ordinary, but of exceptional men; and just as there is 'no excellent beauty without some strangeness in the proportions', so there is no exceptional man without some strangeness in his physical constitution. It may lie, this strangeness, only in an increased, an unusual power to resist strain; that unusual power must be analysed and weighed. Modern science has shown that our surroundings exercise an influence not only on our minds but on our bodies also; that the coal-heaver, by dint of carrying heavy sacks upon his back, experiences a hardening of the spine, so that the soft parts between certain vertebrae become ossified into one solid bone. How far, we may ask ourselves, does a similar process result in the brain, as the result of the lifelong practice of an art or science? *That* cannot yet be measured; but other things can. We can trace an aptitude becoming a predilection and then a talent; we can show how dislike extends into prejudice and thence to aberration; we can show what resistances were weakened to compensate for the exceptional strength displayed elsewhere.

Yet the task of the biographer is not ended even here. His first duty, I have shown, is to be truthful, to understand, and then reflect his understanding; his second, perhaps even more difficult, is to be interesting. By that loose word 'interesting' I mean that his work must conform to the laws of aesthetics, which are unwritten, but just as potent as other unwritten laws. Why should a biography be presented in bad journalese; or, worse, in ornamented journalese? Is there any reason why biography should not display all the graces of a smooth prose style? There is, on the contrary, every reason why it should; for Truth is but the lesser part of the good writer's task, and we are justified in asking of him, not only the skill of the analyst, but the skill of the artist also. Why should not his words, like Poe's or Swift's, be set in sentences like jewels in a crown? Why should not his sentences build up paragraphs as truly as bricks do a wall? Why should not his paragraphs fit into the chapters as inevitably as the parts of a piece of music? There is no element of tragedy or comedy that the biographer might not, if he could, employ, but alas, even in matter of simple *presentation*, biographical standards are as much at fault as in their aim of complete recording. It is widely believed, as we may see from current and from former practice, that the right way of presenting a life-story is to begin at the beginning and proceed to the end. It is not realized (or we should not be afflicted still by the timeworn chronological formula) that such a method is essentially *undramatic;* and that the biographer must not only select his facts, but also

present them in the most telling order. But what, it
may be asked, *is* the most telling order. There is no
single answer, for there is no invariable rule. The
easiest, and one of many sound ways, is to lift the curtain on a hero fully developed and manifesting the
idiosyncrasies which make him worth writing about, to
follow his career until its end, illustrating meanwhile
the changing of his character with the years; and then,
at the finish, to retrace the steps by which he had
become what, in the first chapter, he was shown as
being. That is one method; there are many others; as
many ways as there are of telling a story. For it must
be borne in mind that biography *is* the telling of a story
—of a *life*-story; and differs from fiction only in this,
that whereas the novelist must confine his plot within
the boundary of *probability*, the biographer must observe
the boundary of *fact*. The difference between is not as
vast as it may seem, for, if the matter be considered, it
will be seen that even the novelist is not really free to
choose his plot at all. His own character dictates his
characters to him; he may seem to represent all men,
but in effect he represents himself; and the canon of his
work, if rightly considered, is a single book. The point
is difficult, and need not be stressed; what we must
remember is that the biographer, if he has not an equal,
has still quite definitely a *certain* freedom of choice. If
religious politics do not interest him, he need not write
the life of Mr. Gladstone; if he is revolted by Imperialism, there is no reason why he should select Cecil
Rhodes; and if he has views on morality in literature, he
can leave Aretino to those who lack them. A biographer
should choose his subject as a dandy chooses his suit,
remembering cut and tone as much as texture; and his

subjects should fit his talent as the suit fits the dandy's body: exquisitely. The right length is hardly less important than the right fit. Continuity of interest, totality of impression, have been called the first elements of art; and how can they be spread over three volumes? Books, like rose-bushes, are improved by skilful pruning; to omit is as important as to mention. Poe and Quiller-Couch have shown that *Paradise Lost*, like all epics, loses by its length, and is read in effect, even by its admirers, as a collection of short poems. What Milton could not do with such a theme, the biographical writer may well be chary of attempting; and unless he has such anecdotes as Boswell's with which to beguile the reader, the excellence of brevity is his safest guide.

But, it may be urged, if biography is to be so largely a matter of art, so dramatic in form and colour, is there not a danger that the biographer, to get a better picture, will heighten or invent, distort the truth? I do not think so. The artistic conscience has its own honesty, and the true biographer will accept the convention of truth cheerfully, content with his medium, undismayed because his tool is an etching needle and not a scrubbing brush.

With the record, considered purely as record, I have no quarrel whatsoever. The *Dictionary of National Biography*, and similar works with no aesthetic intention beyond that of neatness, fulfil a useful and valuable purpose. Nor would I discourage the valet or disciple from writing reminiscences of their masters. Such documentary evidence is part of the material which the ideal biographer, when he comes, will sort and review. Without information no biography can be written; and even when the source of origin is tainted, it has some importance. These 'Diaries' and 'Memoirs' are raw material; but they should not be confused with the finished product; they are biographical sources, not biography.

One more element of biographical tradition must be mentioned: that of attitude; and here, too, tradition has gone far astray. The biographies of the past seem to have been composed by men so consciously and aggressively virtuous that they moralized or omitted from their books any actions that seemed in any way indecent, eccentric, or even suspicious. This reticence, which sometimes suggests more than truth would reveal, as in the case of Swinburne, is perhaps a legacy from those monkish chroniclers who wrote the earliest English lives, and haunts us still. It seems to be thought that the memory of a great man is in some dark way damaged if it is recorded that he drank too much, was unfaithful to his wife, or suffered from an unstable mind. When such circumstances have been so plain that not even resolute hypocrisy could hide them, they have been sentimentalized in a scented cloud of romantic gush. From these absurd scruples we are gradually being freed by the growth of scientific knowledge, which is teaching even biographers that heavy drinking is usually a symptom of some hidden need, and that even the normal man is mentally unstable when fatigued. The biographical writer of the future will be entirely free to use or discard, by his own standards, any part of the information available concerning his subject. What those standards will be I have endeavoured to show; and these speculations are at once confirmed and illustrated by the emergence of a group of writers who do, whatever their shortcomings, proclaim by practice that biography is not memorial journalism, but a form of art, and that it is as much entitled as the modern novel to openness of expression. In his astute and well-informed monograph, *The Development of English Biography*, Mr. Harold Nicolson finds the first hints of this new biographical attitude in the irony of Froude's *Carlyle*, and the detached tolerance of *Father and Son*. With these ascriptions we cannot quarrel; and the experimental significance of *Eminent Victorians* is equally beyond dispute. In the biographies of recent years written under Mr. Strachey's influence, faulty though they are, the faults are no longer those of a restrictive tradition, but the initial errors of an untried medium. Is it undue optimism to think that the evil traditions of recording, directness, and reticence are almost ended, and that a new life will begin for biography with their death? Surely we can reason here by analogy from other arts and sciences. When radium counts its martyrs, painting its masters; when we consider the devotion of Balzac and Flaubert, the electrifying passion of Dickens, even the lifelong humanitarian insistence of Galsworthy, is it too much to imagine that biographers *must* arise who will rival these masters in art, assiduity, and honesty? If we believe so, we may take Mr. Strachey as the forerunner of the biographer of the future, who, though not unmindful of learning, will not be a pure scholar, for the scholar is more interested in scholarship than humanity. Nor will art alone, not even the art of writing, claim his sole devotion. Eternally curious, he will know men and books and cities; possess the quick assimilative promptness of the legal mind, and the judicial balancing calm of that mind also; be avid of personality, and rate

men as what they are, rare and curious flowers of
character, interesting both when they conform and
when they differ from the general standards of law
and virtue. If he accomplish all these things, and
possess as well a sense of the theatre and a sense of
style, he may even, in his own right, deserve a brief
biography.

EXPERIMENT IN BIOGRAPHY

By OSBERT BURDETT

THE youngest but one of the forms of literature, the art of biography has had from the first a struggle to define its own aim and to maintain its independence. To record the life of a man from birth to death, truthfully, vividly, and with grace might seem an aim sufficiently simple and interesting. Is not the desire to hear a story instinctive? Is there not peculiar interest in any human story that is true? The end seems so obvious, the limitations so plain, that we might expect no greater room for experiment than in the parallel art of portrait-painting. As you must have heard, however, from the lecture to which this is the successor, this simple view of biography would have seemed extravagant and unwarrantable to past ages, and is, in fact, a modern conception. The study and presentment of a human character, with its contradictions and its failures, with its inner conflict of aim with impulse and its outer struggle between circumstance and temperament, has rarely been the object of biographers. To understand in short why experiment in biography is not a purely technical subject, not a discussion of what used to be called the arts of rhetoric, we have to recall that biography has been dominated by moral theories, from which it has not yet escaped, and that experiment in it has usually proved to be the unconscious instinct of some artist working in rebellion against the prevailing theory.

The instinct of curiosity, strange as this appears, has rarely been the biographer's motive. Biographers have preferred, and often still prefer, to use their subject as

M

an illustration, to make of him an example or a warning, in a word to subordinate his figure to some preconceived purpose of their own. So strong is this temptation that progress in the art can scarcely be observed. Instead we note, and certainly till the time of Boswell, periodic attempts to present (to the scandal of the age) a living portrait without timidity or favour in a persistent tendency to blur the truth, to suppress intimate detail, and to commemorate the subject as the embodiment or contradiction of some current ideal. Nor was Boswell's great example decisive. Within fifty years the example that he set had ceased to be a potent influence. The old wooden idol of Dagon was on his legs again.

When therefore we consider the art of biography and ask what experiment is possible to it, we find that all experiments have been protests against the stock figure, and of late years as much concerned to hold the particular figure lately in vogue up to ridicule as to recapture a living personality. When whitewash is replaced by tar and feathers, a faithful portrait is still to seek. That this should be true of biography in a moment of revival shows how poor are the traditions of the art, how rarely is it pursued from disinterested motives, how much it still lives under the shadow of the lying epitaph, the spiteful reaction, the empty features of the waxen figure or the monumental mason's stock in trade.

For a long time biography followed the novel and confined itself to the record of heroes and villains. The notion that the life of any human being, if told truthfully, sympathetically, and with narrative skill, is rich in interest was recognized very slowly. One consequence

was that successful people, in increasing number as the
nineteenth century advanced, had their lives recorded
in solemn volumes, the literary equivalent of the under-
taker's 'immortal' flowers. To have a biography became as necessary as to have a funeral, at which the art
of biography was numbered with the mutes. Beside
the solemn flattery that these compilations involved,
the preference for successful persons and the emphasis
on their success overlooked an important fact. However pleasant success may be to the man who wins it, it
is failure, in the world's reckoning, that ensures the
interest of posterity. Success is never an easy fact to
live down successfully. Indeed, a man or woman's
failure is his biographer's gain, because failure is more
human than success, more human and, therefore, more
interesting.

    The figure of Joan of Arc is more absorbing to us than
Queen Elizabeth because she was not so successful.
Charles I moves our imaginations more than Charles II
for the same reason. The victories of Austerlitz and
Marengo are all very well as episodes, but it is to
St. Helena that Napoleon owes his dignity in the eyes
of history. His fall from power is the most appealing
moment of his life. Elijah, for instance, would be an
impossible subject for biography because he did not
even die, but was carried up to heaven in a chariot.
Doubtless one reason why the life of Moses has lately
been rewritten is that Moses failed to enter the Promised
Land. The life of Poe is richer than that of Tennyson
because Poe did not receive a peerage. The world
naturally averts its eyes from the truth that something
vulgar is essential to success, but the truth is like a
canker in the rose it wears, and the world is in a well-

understood conspiracy to conceal it. It mistrusts its own standards and its own judgements, and we still stand abashed before the old saying: 'When thou doest good unto thyself all men will speak well of thee.' Thus the lives that it has crowned, Johnson's, Nelson's, Wesley's, Sir Walter Scott's, Charlotte Brontë's, Thomas Arnold's, Florence Nightingale's, were all chequered, and such successes as they attained were only the white squares on the chess-board of their stories. The best of these biographies were those that shrank least from the contrast; the worst those that whitewashed out the truth. In the long run we find that defeat has no indignity. The spirit of a man who dies fighting is not defeated, whereas success coarsens every man in its degree.

For a practical people like the English the temptation to glorify success is very great, and this helps to explain why we have no biographical tradition but, instead, a few wonderful books rising like peaks above a plain of mediocrity. The French are happier, and perhaps the most convenient way of approaching recent experiments in English biography is to take the verdict of a modern French writer upon English practice. In his excellent book *The Brontë Sisters*, which was at length translated in 1927, the Abbé Ernest Dimnet says:

'The English are often poor biographers: at the same time sincere and timid (see the quiet suppression by Bishop Wordsworth of his uncle's romance with a French girl, revealed by my friend Emile Legouis in his book *William Wordsworth and Annette Vallon*, Dent, 1922); arranging facts in a confused manner and afraid of losing anything; excellent psychologists, clear-sighted moralists, but unskilful in assembling the features that end by making a finished portrait.'

M. Dimnet misses, you see, the selection, the light and shade, the engaging or pathetic contrasts, the vital contradictions necessary to a lively portrait. Now the first lesson for a biographer to learn is that contradictions are the salt of character, because no generalized idea that we can form embraces all particulars, and it is in the particulars that life and personality exist. This was increasingly forgotten during Queen Victoria's reign, in the middle period of which there grew a recognized ideal of public deportment, the ideal early noted by Dickens in Mr. Dombey and realized with marvellous fidelity by Mr. Gladstone in his maturity and old age. I myself can recall an old gentleman now dead who never attended Divine Service in the country without insisting upon reading the Lessons because to a man of his pretensions this prominence was due. In my undergraduate days there used to be a tailor who on Sundays was an Elder preaching to his sect and on week-days strode to his shop in a black frock-coat and a top hat crowning his wide white whiskers, umbrella tucked under his arm, the embodiment in his sphere also of Gladstonian deportment and dignity. The ideal figure of these two men, widely separated though they were by class and occupation, was also the ideal of biographers. The lives of their subjects were cut to fit it, and any biographer who, like Froude in his portrait of Carlyle, departed from the pattern and tried his hand at a sketch from life, was execrated. He was accused (it was the final argument) of gross errors of taste. The convention of the toga and the robes, which was imposed on sculptors during the first half of the nineteenth century, ruled longer in the field of letters. The convention was prized far more than vivid portraiture.

The idol then worshipped was the image of Respectability and Success.

With one or two exceptions, for biography has always been an art to some one, this convention persisted throughout King Edward's reign. How far the War, which shook the faith of the younger generation in its elders, hastened the inevitable reaction it is hard to say, but at any rate it was not till 1918 that the convention was exploded. In the May of that year was published Mr. Lytton Strachey's *Eminent Victorians*, a book which by common consent introduced, or rather imported, a more concise, detached, personal, and artistically planned conception of biography. To understand the intentions of the author, and the convention from which he was reacting, some sentences from his preface may be quoted:

'I hope, however, that the following pages may prove to be of interest from the strictly biographical no less than from the historical point of view. . . . The art of biography seems to have fallen on evil times in England. We have had, it is true, a few masterpieces, but we have never had, like the French, a great biographical tradition; we have had no Fontenelles and Condorcets, with their incomparable *éloges*, compressing into a few shining pages the manifold existences of men. . . . Those two fat volumes, with which it is our custom to commemorate the dead—who does not know them with their ill-digested masses of material, their slipshod style, their tone of tedious panegyric, their lamentable lack of selection, detachment, of design? . . . How many lessons are to be learnt from them! But it is hardly necessary to particularize. To preserve, for instance, a becoming brevity—a brevity which excludes everything that is redundant and nothing that is significant—that, surely, is the first duty of a biographer. The second, no less surely, is to maintain his own freedom of spirit. It is not his business to be complimentary; it is his business to lay bare the facts of the case, as he understands them . . . impartially and without ulterior intentions.'

There are valuable reminders here, but not enough, or the lesson would have been better learnt by Mr. Strachey's imitators. Human character, we are shown, should be the biographer's quarry. What a man was is infinitely more important to us than anything which he did, or than the success which attended him. No one complains that Pepys left out of his diary his useful work for the Navy. On the contrary, he is cherished and honoured because he confined himself to personal revelations of his tastes, indulgences, and whims. A biography should be a portrait, not a chronicle, though it is possible by judicious selection to record a busy life in a short compass. Proportion is more illuminating than masses of detail. Perhaps because brevity was imposed by the originators, something like a standard was set in the English Men of Letters series which began under the editorship of John Morley in 1878. In that series the aim has been to balance the life and the works of the different authors in a set of short lives. It is appropriate that one principle of the art, the principle of proportion, should have been strictly enforced in the biographies of English authors. Our men of action have not had the same protection, but Mr. Strachey's essays at least proved how much could be accomplished in a little space, even in a life so crowded as that of Florence Nightingale. This experiment of brevity was highly successful.

This book marks a date as definite as Roper's *Life of Sir Thomas More*, Cavendish's *Wolsey*, Johnson's *Lives*, or Boswell's *Johnson;* though fresh in our minds, it must not simply be taken as read. For one thing it led a reaction, and this, which made it a sensation on its appearance, will prove less of a merit in time to come. Artists should not be concerned with actions or reactions. The more they think of their work and the less of its effect on other people, the better their work will be and the more likely to endure. The advantage of having a tradition is that standards are not lost, and, consequently, do not have to be recovered. No time is wasted in rebellion or experiment, though the modulation by which tradition itself is kept alive, and which indeed constitutes development and growth, leaves ample room for surprise and even hostility. Still, such opposition is healthy; the aim and ground-plan at least are there. Now it cannot be denied that there was a strong element of reaction in Mr. Strachey's book. Whatever qualities in himself separated him from Victorian biographers were emphasized, in his own mind, as differences from them. He was picking an artistic quarrel, and not thinking only of the portraits under his hand. Searching round for models and finding few at home, he looked to France and thereby imported a quality which, though precious, was inevitably foreign. Moreover, he happened to possess a gift of irony, and irony is distrusted and disliked in England where the taste for mockery prefers the heavier weapons of Dickensian ridicule or deliberate satire. In England we take our pleasures strenuously, and work even at sport. Thus, already detached from us, Mr. Strachey could not appeal to any sympathy for his method beyond the satisfaction that its contrast might provide. Now the method itself is questionable for biography, because

irony delights to exhibit weakness, and, unless sparingly
used, thereby implies some want of sympathy with
human nature. Though Mr. Strachey owes much to
French literature, he misses, I think, that subtle sympathy which is also a part of the Gallic spirit. While
(as he assures us) he admires Condorcet, he does not
attempt to write *éloges* himself. True, his essays show
a certain sympathy for witty people such as Dr. Johnson,
Horace Walpole, and Madame du Deffand, but he has
not yet chosen any subject whom we feel to be thoroughly
congenial to him. Perhaps nobody is congenial. Perhaps to him, as to Madame du Deffand, every one
becomes a bore at last. He peeps out, one fancies, in
his concluding sentence on this old, aristocratic woman:
'Certainly there is something at once pitiable and
magnificent in such an unflinching perception of the
futilities of living, such an uncompromising refusal to
be content with anything save the one thing that it is
impossible to have. But is there something alarming
too; was she perhaps right after all?' Ashes to ashes!
Mr. Strachey is more in love with analysis than with
portraiture, with his method than with man.

Of that method, which reduces public figures to
human proportions, which rolls away the stone from
whited sepulchres, which detects the feet of clay in
popular idols, to whom every man is a specimen, and
the exhibition of weakness a tonic pleasure, Mr.
Strachey is a master. He could not employ it so well if
he was possessed of other tools. The fact to notice is
this: it is a limited method, and the biographic art that
it produces, excellent in its own kind, is still under the
dominion of a theory, a theory in which truth, portraiture, is not the primary end. The real subject of

Mr. Strachey's books is the earnest ideal that he ridicules. The consequence is that in each of his books we find the same method, of approach, of construction, of peroration even, applied to different characters, not a succession of different men and women. Every biographer has his own style, but the more pronounced the style, the more limited the point of view, the less room is there for human variety. In a word, the criticism that Mr. Strachey has directed is more useful to biography than the fashion that he has set. He has counterattacked the heresy of whitewash. He has not saved his imitators from the equal heresy of tar and feathers. It is useless to look in his works for a gallery of portraits. One passes his turnstile in search of a certain convention which is delightful for its contrast to the lately prevailing mode. How far he is capable of strict biography could only be seen if he wrote the life of some one who had hitherto found no biographer, of some one preferably unknown—so that there would be no legend to overthrow.

I permit myself these qualifications in the interest of our main subject, for clearly experiment in biography would have little meaning for us if the tradition of English biography were vigorous and healthy. Ironic analysis is certainly an experiment, but in the dish that biographers prepare irony should be no more prominent than salt.

The fashion thus set is still in vogue, but it is not worth while to discuss his many imitators in detail. Clearly, however, they would not have their opportunity merely because a better writer has rescued biography from standard dullness. The truth is that biography itself has come into fashion again; apart from sum-

maries of epochs, it seems to be the only popular branch
of history; and, for one reason, that the field of fiction
seems, however deceptively, exhausted. I believe one
cause to be that the novel has become a literary form
tedious to people who are capable of reading anything
else. Just as the newspaper has been found out, and
readers now turn for ideas and information to short
books, so the glut of novels has disgusted those who have
no leisure to sift the few good from the mass of mediocre
novels. Is there any one in this room who does not take
up a new novel, not recommended by some one whose
judgement he can trust, without misgiving? It is not
an unreasonable prejudice. It is a reaction from satiety
with the form. We have all read innumerable disap-
pointing novels, and when they happen to be bad the
horrid and familiar apparatus of the story-teller stares
us in the face. Not every one pauses to analyse the
feeling, so I will give an illustration. If you read old
plays, indeed almost any play written before 1900, does
not your heart sink when you meet the formula on
page one: The curtain rises and the hero is discovered.
. . . If you take up half a dozen novels and compare
their beginnings, you will find that three or four stock
openings are repeated in the same way, and that the
descriptive scenes, the reflective passages, the dialogue,
the love-affair, are repetitions of a kindred formula.
This satiety, I think, has something to do with the
revived interest in biography. Even if a biography
begins with the date of birth, even if the life be dull,
there is some compensation in the thought that the
events really happened, that the bore was a real bore,
and not invented for our amusement.

The field of inferior fancy has been exhausted, and

the appetite for novels seeks a new ground. A man who cannot invent a good story can sometimes tell or retell one in an engaging way. The temptation therefore comes to make the life of a real man the subject of a novel, to apply the method of fiction to a story that at least is true. So far so good. A lively convention is better than a dull one, but unfortunately there is another side to the picture. In the current search after the sprightly and picturesque, there is a tendency to distort and to embroider. In sum, the novel, pretending to be something stricter, is appropriating the biographer's field. The historical novel, once carefully labelled but now a recognized variety, has won its place, and there is no reason why we should not extend the experiment by creating a new class of biographical novels. One notices, however, that the experimenters will not have this. On the contrary, they claim that the distinction between biography and fiction is false, that the novelist is the true biographer. I will give you chapter and verse in a moment, for the heresy is worth notice, and the reasons that prove it to be a heresy are worth attention.

The historical novel practises no deception, for we know that the author's implied claim to omniscience is a convention and no more. The biographical romance is now making the same claim, but, dealing as a rule with some fairly recent personage whose life has already been investigated, we are at once aware, if we are reading critically, of a disparity between the romance and recorded facts. Of a real person of recent date, you cannot make many assertions unsupported by facts and evidence, and the evidence strictly limits your interpretation if your object is to be reliable and true. Now

the object of these romances is to make a true story
entertaining, and for the entertainment the author
pretends to a perception of motives, an insight into
character, perfectly justifiable concerning an imaginary
person but less justifiable concerning a real one. A
biographer must confess his ignorance when he is
ignorant, for his object is not to entertain but to tell the
truth. This difference of object distinguishes biography
from romancing, and the distinction should be borne
in mind even by those who welcome, as we all may, the
new experiment of romances with a biographical root.

The French have accepted the distinction cheerfully.
M. André Maurois, though he favours the heresy that
I have noticed, when in 1924 he made a great success
with a novel of which Shelley was the hero, was careful
to call his book *Ariel: a Shelley romance*. Thus no one
could mistake it for a life of Shelley. It was a graceful
and sympathetic sketch, with more sauce than substance,
for the author was free to be as picturesque as he chose.
You will remember that, in so far as it was a life, it
omitted Shelley's poetry; enough to prove that it was
romantic to the verge of fiction! The plan was proving
popular in France, for in 1925 there began to be issued
a series of similar romances on the lives of French
authors: Le roman des grands existences, of which
M. René Benjamin's *La Vie prodigieuse de Honoré de
Balzac* was the first and perhaps the best. A translation
of this book is now available, so that the English
reader can judge for himself how far biography is confused with fiction. It may be said at once that the
method would lose its charm if events were invented.
That mistake is too obvious to make. The procedure is
for the romancer to assume the novelist's complete

understanding of his character, to embroider his life with scraps of conversation, sometimes real but sometimes invented, with the ascription of motives, the object of which is to lend vividness to the picture. Unless we regard these lives as romances founded on fact, we are apt to be critical of assumptions that we know cannot be proved. Indeed they are often invented to fill gaps in our knowledge. But a fault in a biography may be an opportunity in a romance; and, were not some of these romances offered to us in the guise of biographies, there would be no reason to demur. The point must be impressed because the experimenters are confusing it, not by accident, but in set terms.

Last autumn M. Maurois defined his attitude to the romances of which he is the happy exponent in a book called *Aspects de la Biographie*. There he explained that biography was a branch of psychology, and resolved itself into an attempt to reconstruct the personality. He went on to imply that there is no real difference between biography and fiction. It is timely to recall that he is a novelist himself. In other words, he would have us believe that intuition is infallible, a theory natural to a novelist but one that no biographer would admit. It is a dangerous mistake for a biographer to make, since it makes the author more important than his subject. The method teaches us more about him than of the man who occupies his attention. The author who relies mainly on intuition will necessarily dominate the page, whereas in a good biography the subject will fill it and make us feel that we are face to face with him. While we are glad to concede this licence to a novelist, since he is the sole authority for his facts and inferences, we distrust it in a biographer. Moreover, in a biography too complete and finished a portrait defeats its own aim, for human characters are obscure and puzzling, and some loose ends in a biography convey this oddity best. A perfectly finished biography has an air of being machine-made. Intuition has its place, but we require also fairness, not to the subject only, but to the materials, gaps and all.

Before all else, a biography must be reliable. To pretend to knowledge that does not exist is only less bad than to suppress evidence. Because they have chosen the same subject, let us glance at M. Maurois's and Edward Dowden's respective lives of Shelley. The shorter is the more entertaining, though it leaves the poet out. It can be read by one to whom Shelley was a romantic scapegrace and no more. To many people, however, Shelley is still much more than this. They have begun with the poetry, and under its spell have become possessed by a passionate curiosity about its author. They want to know all that can be known of him; they want the truth. Let them read both books. To which will they turn when they are in perplexity; to which will they go for information; on which will they rely wherever the two may conflict? There can be only one answer: on Dowden's. The reason has nothing to do with the merits of either author. It is that Dowden wrote a biography, M. Maurois a romance, and that a romance is one thing and a biography another.

Even the experiment of romantic biography has its limitations. You will notice that it choses instinctively romantic characters. Swift, Shelley, Byron, Disraeli, Napoleon, Moses, are types. We have not yet seen it appropriating Boswell, Trollope, Ben Jonson, though these comparatively prosaic people are equally attractive to the biographer. The happiest field for romantic biography is the obscure and remote past, when curiosity must rely upon imagination in the place of knowledge. Indeed, romance can be described as an agreeable substitute for truth. When a novelist like Mrs. Atherton writes a story round Aspasia or Alcibiades we are grateful, for she clothes a skeleton of facts with a tissue of imagination. Mr. George Moore did a similar service with his romance upon Heloise and Abelard. Indeed, the true domain of fancy is beyond the border of fact, though fancy can be employed on facts if the difference be kept clear. Many such subjects will occur to you. Think of an imaginary life of Socrates by Xantippe, a life of Phryne, a romance entitled *Ann Hathaway's Husband* with that lady's diary for its source!

The experiment offered to biography by the intuitive method really runs into a different and stricter field.

Within the limits set by fidelity, the method of the biographer is not fixed, and here we pass into an experiment that has scarcely yet been tried. During the past fifty years a new science, still in its infancy, has appeared under the forbidding name of analytic psychology. The term is most convenient when not too narrowly defined, for the definitions differ. For our purpose it may be termed the analysis of human motives, the dissection of human personality, of the way our minds work, of the nature of our impulses, of the manner in which human beings react to their interior stresses and to external circumstances, of the evidence provided by our dreams. Dreams are now held to be purely subjective in content. This psychology seeks to answer such questions as why a man is habitually self-confident or melancholy, why timid or shy, irritable, criminal, or a stammerer, whenever the reason is not clear. Since we are most curious of eccentric characters, it is eccentrics or the eccentricities of ordinary beings that chiefly engage psychology. Blake and Nietzsche have evoked many essays from the professionals, and there is a streak in all men that can be helpfully studied in this way. The first thing that psychology teaches us is not to run away from contradictions, and the second is that contrary impulses, aversion and attraction, often proceed from the same source. A ferocious chastity is now a trait as suspicious as its opposite. We cannot tie complacent labels any more. This method, being highly technical, has not yet produced, so far as I know, any full biography, but it may come. It has been applied by an expert to Hamlet with results startling to the profane. Sooner or later we shall have psycho-analysts among biographers. These, you observe, will be tributaries influencing the main stream, providing new aspects for study, not absorbing biography itself. To this we must add the purely medical method which has already given us, special studies apart, some books intended for general readers on the part played by their diseases in the lives and policies of English kings! It is hardly necessary to discuss the number of particular approaches that advancing specialism in other fields of knowledge offers to biographers. What angle is there from which a man may not be studied? In truth a romantic interest is no less special than a scientific one, and strict biography, the art of combining a truthful portrait with skilled and impersonal presentment, will continue. The experiments enrich our means, but they do not replace

N

our primary conception, that biography is the history of an individual as a branch of humane letters.

When all has been said, biography, like other arts, is more elusive in its theory than its practice. If a writer has an instinct for the form and a grip on human character, the biography that he produces will be more acceptable than any theory. The practitioner and the professor are rightly diffident when they trespass upon each other's field. Conversation, and then correspondence, remain the biographer's best materials, and no experiment with these, no theory of presentment, can vie with a sympathetic imagination. The evidence of this is respect for truth, abundant human sympathy, a determination neither to praise nor to blame, but to leave the reader free to draw his own inferences from the complex characteristics presented to him. Insight into character is the reward of those who present without bias the jumble of actions and ascertainable motives, good and bad, the sum of which is a living human being. A judge or an advocate will weigh one fact against another, but the biographer knows that the life of his portrait is in proportion to the amount of light and shade. By showing Johnson in all his moods and in many different circumstances, Boswell remains the greatest of experimenters, and because his method is arduous and exacts an extraordinary degree of devotion it has scarcely had an imitator. The real experiment, therefore, would be to employ the same assiduity and to take the same amount of pains.

TRADITION IN CRITICISM

By REBECCA WEST

THE literary criticism of every age is only the application
to the particular instance of the theories about literature
which are current at that moment. One can, therefore,
get a rough idea of what literary criticism has been like
in Europe through the centuries by tracing the growth
and supersession of the various theories of the purpose
and technique of literature which were begun by
Aristotle. For one may as well in a survey as brief as
this pass over the views of Plato who considered art as
simply an imitation of the universe, and therefore a
frivolous waste of time. And in a survey as brief one
may as well pass over also Aristotle's (384–322 B.C.)
principle of the Unities, by which he laid down that in
a drama there should be unity of place, unity of time,
unity of action, partly for the reason that others better
than ourselves (for example, Shakespeare) have passed
it over; and partly for the reason that considered in its
right place in *The Poetics* it amounts to nothing more
than a statement that observance of these conditions
seems to suit the Greek drama, which was the only form
of tragedy that Aristotle (for most excellent reasons
arising out of time and space) could know. It is more to
the point to go to his definition of Tragedy.

'Tragedy, then, is an imitation of an action that is serious,
complete, and of a certain magnitude; in language embellished with each kind of artistic ornament, the several
kinds being found in separate parts of the play; in the form
of action, not of narrative; through pity and fear effecting
the propagation of these emotions.'

Now, though Aristotle is one of the few people whom one can dislike with as fresh intensity as if they were in the next room though they died a couple of thousand of years ago, one must admit that this definition is one of the most extraordinary achievements of the human mind. With very little material in front of him, with virtually nothing to go upon in the way of previous discussions of the subject (as one can see from the simplicity with which Plato faced the problem), Aristotle produced a definition of art which has been found to hold water when it has been tested by any of the works of art that have been produced in the twenty succeeding centuries. Art has some sort of correspondence with the external world we see around us, that is, it has to have some relation with reality. The part of reality it refers to must have some sort of importance, or it will not hold our attention. The next clause—'in language embellished with each kind of artistic ornament, the several kinds being found in several parts of the play'—betrays the philosopher with the passion for putting things into categories, and leaving nothing on its own. Practice has proved that there is no reason why a play should not enjoy complete stylistic purity, and be all in one manner, or why it should not employ different sorts of artistic ornament with much greater audacity of fusion than Aristotle suggests. But we find ourselves in undebatable ground with the assertion that in tragedy we must have action, not narrative. For that is a presentation, in the terms of the drama with which Aristotle was dealing, that whatever happens in a work of art must be proved to happen under the audience's eye, that they must be convinced of its reality. And the last clause—'through pity and fear effecting the propagation of these

emotions'—states the fact that in a work of art it is an
artist's business to communicate to the spectators the
emotion that has been caused in him by certain
material.

Now, every work of art that one can think of comes
more or less within that definition. The most startling
example of that is the art-form which is farthest from
Aristotle's world both in time and in spirit: the modern
novel. It is obvious to all of us that a novel cannot be
a satisfactory novel unless it refers sufficiently to the
external world (which is the common property of both
the author and ourselves) for us to get a clue to what he
is writing about; but this material which has been drawn
from life must be given a twist before it becomes a work
of art, parts of it must be analysed, in fact the characters
must be clearly drawn. The readers will not be convinced
that what the author says about these characters is true
unless they are exhibited displaying the characteristics
which he alleges in action, and unless the author makes
his readers feel what he did when he contemplated his
subject, they will feel nothing, in which case they will
justly consider the time they have spent listening to him
as wasted, or they will disagree, and become eaten up
with controversial irritation. This is but one example
of the prescience of Aristotle, but this is his great contribution to criticism: to have known, when only a
minute fraction of literature had come into being, almost
as much as to why and how it came into being as the
best brains have ever worked out since.

There is nothing else so important in the writings
of the ancients on this subject; which indeed mainly
fall under the head of Rhetoric, an art which was of
supreme importance in its time because it dug the

foundations of style, but which dealt with such matters of detail that it is hard to pick out any particular illustration of the benefits literature derived from its statements of the previously unestablished. But there comes presently Longinus who established something that we may find it rather hard to believe ever needed to be established, and that is the power of beauty. In his treatise *De Sublimitate* he lays down more positively than had ever been done before (though the rhetoricians laid stress on the fact that decorum of presentation made an argument more acceptable) on the effect of beautiful language on the mind. 'For beautiful words are the true and peculiar light of the mind,' he says. He gave beauty its prestige: a prestige which, however, was not to be of much use to it in the Dark Ages that followed. For there was little if any lay literature during that period, and it was another kind of beauty, a beauty sanctioned by theology, that had her day then. And before pure beauty could get back Dante had to establish the principle that a man had to write in his mother-tongue, and loose the limbs of the creative spirit from the swaddling-bands imposed on it by the obligation to write in Latin, a language which they learned in a scholar's mood and which fixed that mood in them when they used it. In the *De Vulgari Eloquio* he teases out the question of how a man should write if he wants to record his spontaneous reactions to the world he lives in without using the coarser speech that is used among the common folk. This test point of view was natural to an Italian, whose language was specially liable to such degradation in the mouths of the vulgar by the tendency to slur consonants or omit final consonants, and so form dialects incomprehensible outside a small district. His solution of the

Illustrious Vernacular put Europe on its way to the modern literature we know.

That literature had not too easy a path, for remember pure beauty was handicapped by her lonely state and her lack of theological sanction. So you have as the first considerable work of criticism in England after the Renaissance (dealing with literature as a thing in itself apart from scholarship), Sir Philip Sidney's (1554–86) *Defence of Poetry*, which bases its case on the usefulness of poetry as a means of communicating useful knowledge and remembering the virtues. His argument was of course not completely candid. Evidence abounds that Sir Philip Sidney had a proper respect for poetry as a thing in itself and would have liked poetry anyhow. But there were a great many people then as now who do not understand that we should encourage art, not in order that it should confirm our existing morality, but that it should run ahead of us and illuminate experience in such a way that we can amplify and modify that morality. In fact the Roman Catholic Church felt so strongly on the subject that the censorship of books was an ever-present concern of hers from the moment the new literature began to be. But there was, as well as a moral reaction against the wakening literature of Europe, an aesthetic one. This took the form of a desire that writers of that day should tame down their crude and violent forces by subjecting themselves to the discipline of classic order. The chief advocate of this was Ben Jonson (1573–1637), who argued that his contemporaries should purge themselves of their tendency to heated exuberance by imitating the chastity and sense of proportion that distinguished the Greek writers. His advocacy illustrates the curious freak of

human nature by which we admire our opposites, for
of all the greater Elizabethans none seems so curiously
crabbed and lacking in spontaneousness or ability to
manage his own gifts as Ben Jonson.

A generation later that underrated genius Dryden
(1631–1700) was to answer him, and say that it would
be too amazing a coincidence if two peoples, so widely
separated in space and time as the Greeks and the
English, should so closely resemble each other that their
most personal product, their art, could find the same
forms suitable. If English poets needed to discipline
themselves, the constraints must be shaped to fit their
English spirit. He went on to discuss what art might be,
and came to the conclusion that it was imitation, with
a difference, and that difference consists of touches applied by the artist for the purpose of creating delight in
the spectator. He calls the faculty which leads to the
application of the right touches the imagination. And
he left matters pretty much at that. But he and the age
in which he wrote left the conception of imagination
about for the rationalist eighteenth century to use as
a peg for its theories. It did some very odd things about
it. Addison, for example, believed that it was almost
literally an image: that the artist remembered a certain
number of sensory perceptions, arranged them in the
same order which they had occupied in life or another
one, and then expressed opinions about them. And
when he was asked why this proceeding gave anybody
any pleasure he said God made people so that it did:
which is cheating. Addison was, in fact, an excellent
critic; he gave the old English ballads due credit for one
thing. But in his generalizations he is a long way behind
Aristotle. So is Burke (1729–97) in his essay *The Sublime*

and the Beautiful, which virtually identifies the pleasure given by art as the pleasure of recognition. It is no wonder that the specific literary criticisms of this age strike one as remarkably poor. The qualities which made it a great age for speculative thought made it a sad one for artistic judgement. It seems to us almost incredible that Dr. Johnson's (1709–84) *Lives of the Poets* should ever have excited anything but derision. He might be excused for failure to appreciate Dante, since they were temperamentally at the opposite poles; but the silliness of his comments on Milton (1608–74) ('Surely no man could have fancied that he read *Lycidas* with pleasure, had he not known his author') is so alien from the splendid good sense of his general demeanour that one perceives that there is some element in the situation compelling him to talk nonsense. That element is the insistence of his century that everything should be discussed—a picture, a poem, a play—in the same manner in which the truth of a scientific proposition can be disputed—is what it says true or not? Does the image appear the same length as its original in the water? Did Milton and his friend in fact drive in a field and both together hear 'What time the grey-fly winds her sultry horn, Battening their flocks with the fresh dews of night?'

Something had to happen to the theory of criticism; and there appeared the neo-classic, who held up Greece and Rome as models to the late eighteenth century. It is one of the most admirable things in Mr. Scott-James's book, *The Making of Literature,* that he points out that the neo-classical writers knew little or nothing of the classics, that the Greece and Rome of their imagination had nothing to do with the Greece and Rome that had actually existed. We can get an idea of

what happened from our own London architecture.
The Adam brothers went to Italy, saw some vast
deserted palaces that had been built to house thousands,
accepted that as the scale of the ancients' private
houses, and came back and built the enormous man-
sions and spacious terraces which would have amazed
the teeming populations that lived in each other's laps
in Rome or Pompeii. This is very much what happened
in literature, when the neo-classicists urged the young
writers to adopt a classicism which had nothing whatsoever to do with the virility of Homer, the passion of
Aeschylus and Sophocles and Euripides, the impertinent
grace of Horace, the freshness of Catullus, the imaginative vision of Virgil. It embodies a constraining formalism which might be suggested to a schoolboy by
scansion of Latin verse, but could hardly be identified
by riper scholars. This point of view inspired much
eighteenth-century French criticism; and it was revolted
against at the middle of the century by the Germans,
chiefly by Wincklemann, who was also a neo-classicist,
but went back to the real Greece and Rome. I must
confess, however, that he had a flair for the worst of the
real Greece and Rome, and that he represented the
great artists of antiquity as engaged in propaganda for
a certain kind of robust, morally certified beauty, rather
than as the impartial workers who use beauty as a part
of their technique but not as a conscious end that they
were.

Then came Lessing (1729–81), who was a far greater
man. He looked at the problem of literature from a
really new point of view. He saw that the neo-classics
who kept on telling the artist that they needed to prune
their work into definite shapes were not recommending

the kind of restraint the artist most requires: which is restraint in choosing his material. In *Laocoon* he discusses what sort of material is necessary for different forms of art; a picture, a statue, a poem. Virtually this works out to a discussion of by what means artists can impress the content of this subject on the spectator's attention by other than bare factual statement, and thence to an analysis of the spectator's attention. That is to say, he paved the way for modern psychological criticism. Of which, though he would probably have denied it, and though the men of sense in his day would have laughed the idea to scorn, William Blake was the first and greatest example. With something of a D. H. Lawrence's explosively epigrammatic quality he wished all the scholists—particularly poor Sir Joshua Reynolds who had padded all round Europe measuring pictures to find out what proportion of light and shade in a picture made a really good picture—at the bottom of the tenth Purgatory to the left in his mystical system. He declared that rules based on a study of the external forms of the world were bunkum. He had a right to draw what he saw; and that was not the same as the images that the external forms imprinted on his retina. And considering how every such image is immediately taken charge of by the associative faculty, and given its place in a private world the mind has built up for itself, there is no doubt that he was right.

It is curious that Wordsworth's reaction against neo-classicism, though just as profound as Blake's, led him in the opposite direction. He says, 'Let me represent without distortion the forms of the external world, selected and beheld by the operation of strong feelings'; which, in turn, was operated by a unifying creative faculty which he goes on naming and renaming under the impression that he is defining it. It is what Shelley claims to be his motive-power, and boldly calls inspiration. Their aesthetic theory was comically poor, in view of their aesthetic practice; and the contrast was even greater in the case of Coleridge, whose *Biographia Literaria* is full of good things, but leads up to nothing but a restatement of the existence of inspiration, which he called under the name of the Esemplastic Imagination. This is really no advance on Aristotle. For Aristotle defines Tragedy; others ask what makes men create Tragedy; the aesthetics of the soul answer, a Unifying Creative Faculty Inspiration, an Esemplastic Imagination. But when one questions, what is this Unifying Creative Faculty, this Inspiration, this Esemplastic Imagination, the only answer is, it is what makes men create Tragedy. Such repetitiousness is constantly found in the writings of Goethe on criticism. But a new and valuable point that Coleridge made is that the pleasure given by art is 'immediate': it exists independently of the pleasure given by the satisfaction of any other appetite. This is a complete abandonment of the Defence of Poetry attitude to art.

Meanwhile, there was emerging a new kind of specific criticism which was the successful practice of what Dr. Johnson had failed to do in *The Lives of the Poets*. It worked on the theory that the critic can do a service to literature by analysing the external forces which have acted upon the individual character of an author and seeing how they have affected his choice of his material and his treatment of it. The past master of this, who cared but little for his greater contemporaries' concentration on abstract theory (though he also dealt with it), was

William Hazlitt (1778–1830). He settles down in front of his subject, and says, 'You see he writes this or that way, because he is this or that kind of man, and has been affected by this or that personality and this or that movement.' Since he was a man of the most exquisite conceivable sensibility, with a comprehensive mind that could take in his age at a glance, and had a tripping and expressive style, the results of this method were most successful. To read his essay on Wordsworth in *The Spirit of the Age* is to find oneself for ever after much better able to find his way about the poet's genius. And a little later on the other side of the Channel, Sainte-Beuve (1804–69) was to do the same, with a great deal more certitude as to why he used this method. He thought that the critic was a kind of natural historian of genius and the talents that in their extreme development rise to genius; that one ought to be able to take a writer to the critic and say, 'Now, what is this?' just as if one catches a bird one cannot identify one takes it to the experts at the Zoo or the South Kensington Natural History Museum. In this he failed, of course. The mental species are too mutable. But he succeeded marvellously in his investigation of the particular instances he chose. Benjamin Constant's *Adolphe* is, of course, one of the great novels of the world. But the interest it arouses in one is enormously increased if one reads Sainte-Beuve's study of the timid and tortured creature who wrote it. It is an excellent thing to have Sainte-Beuve's *Causeries du Lundi* in the house and dip into them whenever the supply of contemporary literature fails: because every paper contains a complete analysis of a human being and the relation between his personality and his work. It is also an excellent thing to have as many volumes as

you can afford of Taine's work, which was published
about the same time. Taine wrote as delightfully as
Sainte-Beuve and he developed still further the theory
of the determinist nature of literature—which denied
that man was a free agent in choosing the literature he
would create, which claimed that that would be determined by the kind of man he was and the external
forces that had affected him. He practically identified
the age and its literature. This was practically a reversion to the ideas of John Dryden who had insisted on
the organic relationship between a nation and its
literature. It was a point of view that had of course
fallen out of sight very much during the sway of the
neo-classicists on the one hand and on the other hand of
the believers in inspiration. The contribution that Taine
made was, however, really more to history than to
literary criticism: as can be judged from a fine passage
in *Les Origines de la France Contemporaire*.

'Consider in turn, during the same period, in France and
in England, where it is most extensively used, the romance,
a sort of mirror everywhere transportable, the best adapted
to reflect all phases of nature and of life. After reading the
series of English novelists, Defoe, Richardson, Fielding,
Smollett, Sterne, and Goldsmith down to Miss Burney and
Miss Austen, I am familiar with England in the eighteenth
century; I have encountered clergymen, country gentlemen,
farmers, innkeepers, sailors, people of every condition in
life, high and low; I know the details of fortunes and of
careers, how much is earned, how much is expended, how
journeys are made and how people eat and drink: I have
accumulated for myself a file of precise biographical events,
a complete picture in a thousand scenes of an entire community, the amplest stock of information to guide me
should I wish to frame a history of this vanished world. On

reading a corresponding list of French novelists, the younger Crebillon, Rousseau, Marmontel, Laclos, Restif de la Breton, Louvet, Madame de Staël, Madame de Genlis, and the rest, including Mercier and even Mme Cottin, I scarcely take any notes; all precise and instructive little facts are left out; I find civilities, polite acts, gallantries, mischief-making, social dissertations, and nothing else. They carefully abstain from mentioning money, from giving me figures, from describing a wedding, a trial, the administration of a piece of property; I am ignorant of the situation of a curate, of a rustic noble, of a resident prior, of a steward, of an intendant. Whatever relates to a province or to the rural districts, to the bourgeoisie or to the shop, to the army or to a soldier, to the clergy or to convents, to justice or to the police, to business or to housekeeping, remains vaguely in my mind or is falsified; to clear up any point I am obliged to recur to that marvellous Voltaire who, on laying aside the great classic coat, finds plenty of elbow room and tells all. On the organs of society of vital importance, on the practices and regulations that provoke revolutions, on feudal rights and seigniorial justice, on the mode of recruiting and governing monastic bodies, on the revenue measures of the provinces, of corporations and of trade-unions, on the tithes and the *corvées*, literature provides me with scarcely any information. Drawing-rooms and men of letters are apparently its sole material. The rest is null and void. Under the good society that is able to converse France appears perfectly empty.'

He gave literature prestige as not an ornament but a function of life, but he did not do as much to explain it as Hazlitt and Sainte-Beuve. English literature owes them a great debt of gratitude, though their kind of criticism brought trouble with it because it afforded scope for innumerable offences when practised by persons less gifted and less honest. When Hazlitt wrote:

'Mr. Gifford was originally bred to some handicraft, he afterwards contrived to learn Latin, and was for some time an usher in a school, till he became a tutor in a nobleman's family. The low-bred, self-taught man, the pedant, and the dependant on the great contribute to form the Editor of the *Quarterly Review*. He is admirably qualified for this situation, which he has held for some years, by a happy combination of defects, natural and acquired: and in the event of his death, it will be difficult to provide him a suitable successor.' He was more than justified, since Mr. Gifford was the sturdy reviewer who had begged Mr. Keats to give up this art of poetry for which he had no aptitude. But many of his literary descendants would write similar sentences for no other reason than that they thought Mr. Gifford made rather more money than they did, or had got them blackballed for the Savile Club, or some such ungodly reason. There have, however, been many worthy descendants such as Mr. Edmund Gosse and Mr. Desmond McCarthy.

The next critic in England was Matthew Arnold; and I am going to be bold and say that he was a man of immense usefulness to his age and hardly any for ours. He upheld the claims of culture against the spirit of the times which demanded that everything should be practical and insisted that the Parthenon should be regarded as a small thing compared with a steam-engine. But he was a man of very poor taste. He carried in his mind a sense of what people of refined taste have admired in prose and poetry through the ages, and that made him a good guide to the past. But his Lectures on the Translation of Homer are profoundly shocking, since they contain a serious suggestion that idiosyn-

cratic poetry should be translated into cliches, because
cliches represented people's notions of the picturesque.
This is by no means the only shock before those who
examine his works. Ruskin also served the interests of
art by advocating its claims to importance in face of the
derision of the machine age, but he went back to the
stage of Sir Philip Sidney and the Inquisition in his
anxiety to justify the existence of art by finding a connexion between it and established morality. To this
end he developed a theory which propounded that no
supreme art could be created except by religious men:
and that though irreligious men may create fine art this
is never really great. Also all art must be propagandist,
and directed towards the people, including everybody,
particularly the hewers of wood and drawers of water.
He held this democratic fallacy almost as strongly as
Tolstoy, whose *What is Art?* casts out of the window
Shakespeare and Beethoven because they are not of
immediate practical use to the moujik. It is, of course,
a fallacy because there is no reason why a work of art
should appeal to everybody any more than a garment
should fit everybody. There is every reason why hewers
of wood and drawers of water should have art in their
lives: but there is no reason why people living in different conditions should not also have art in their lives.
Ruskin, however, was a great explorer of art, and re-
commender of it; and often wrote so beautifully himself
that all must be forgiven him.

Walter Pater (1839–94) is a writer who has as much
meaning for our age as for his own. It would be a
sad day when people stopped reading *Marius the Epi-
curean*. In that, and in all his sketches, as well as in
his essays on criticism, he defines the kind of detach-

ment, the cool determination to record reality without perverting it in order to flatter a personal appetite (which gets back to Coleridge's idea of 'immediate' pleasure) which makes the artist; and he rebuts Ruskin's demand that art shall hobble itself by a propagandist aim by pointing out that life would be so much pleasanter if we all adopted this impersonal attitude instead of restricting it to art, that art does an immense moral service simply by popularizing it. Of him one can say with certainty that his criticism will live as long as literature, though he suffered disparagement immediately after his career by the fact that his theory was misunderstood by the public and turned to account by the preposterous people in the 'nineties who talked about Art for Art's sake. They were sound in their contention that art need not be didactic, but they used it as an excuse to perpetrate art that was as poor and woolly as can be. The literary contributions to *The Yellow Book* and *The Savoy* are for the most part pitifully slight.

I draw near the confines of my subject; Mr. Eliot has a right to whatever comes after. But there is a form of criticism (of which, by the way, Mr. Eliot would disapprove and I would not) in which it takes almost the likeness and habits of imaginative work. Addison, Charles Lamb, Leigh Hunt (a writer whose stock has fallen too low; some of his stuff is very nimble), De Quincey, the Liszt of essayists; Leslie Stephen—all these took a book or poem as if it were an experience like any other and wrote a subjective account of it. It seems to me beyond question that some of the developments of this lyric movement are amongst the highest achievements of criticism. George Moore's *Avowals*, in which he writes of Tolstoy and Dostoevsky exactly as if they were imaginary people, explain those characters better than any other criticism. And here is a passage from Proust's *A La Recherche du Temps Perdu*. Bergotte is Anatole France.

'Because of a slight attack of uraemia his doctors had told him to rest. But a critic having said that in the "View of Delft" by Vermeer (lent by the Museum of the Hagen for a Dutch Exhibition), a picture that he adored and thought he knew quite well, there was a tiny bit of yellow wall (which he did not remember) which was so exquisitely painted that it was, if one looked at it by itself, of a self-sufficing beauty like a Chinese work of art. Bergotte ate some potatoes, went out, and visited the Exhibition. As soon as he got to the first steps that he had to climb, he was seized with giddiness. He passed in front of several pictures and had an impression of the staleness and futility of such factitious art, which could make nothing equal to the breezes and sun of a Venetian palace or a simple house by the sea. At last he came to the Vermeer which he remembered more brilliant, more different from everything he knew, but in which, thanks to the critics' article, he remarked for the first time that there were certain little people in blue, that the gravel was pink, and moreover that there was indeed this tiny bit of yellow wall. His giddiness increased; he fixed his eye, like a child who sees a yellow butterfly that it wants to catch, on the bit of yellow wall. "That is how I ought to have written," he said. "My last books are too dry. I ought to have laid on several coats of colour, to have made my sentence a beautiful thing in itself, like that bit of yellow wall." Meanwhile, he was not blind to the serious-ness of his attack of gididness. There appeared to him in a heavenly balance, weighing down one of the scales, his own life, while the other one contained the bit of yellow wall that had been so well painted. He felt he had rashly exchanged the first for the second. "I wouldn't like", he said to himself, "to be among the miscellaneous news of this Exhibition in the evening papers."

'He repeated to himself: "A little bit of yellow wall with a shed, a little bit of yellow wall." Meanwhile he had sunk on to a circular divan; quite suddenly he stopped thinking that life was a game, and, hurrying back to optimism, said to himself, "This is simply indigestion that I've got from underdone potatoes, it isn't anything". A new attack overcame him, he rolled off the divan to the ground, and all the visitors and the custodians hurried up to him. He was dead.'

Proust has throughout the book explained his own character, the 'moi' of the book, so that one knows the personality of the critic, what allowances one ought to make for his bias. He has enlarged on Bergotte, the writer who is a great genius, but who was not of complete integrity: he likes antiques, fripperies, parties, he has lost that attitude which Pater defines as most essential to the artist. In this paragraph we get a flashing vision of the perfect honesty of Vermeer's genius, the dappled dishonesty of Anatole France's genius. This is a very high order of criticism; and it seems to me a novelty on which an age may congratulate itself.

I would like to append a note recommending to all persons interested in this subject *The Making of Literature*, by R. A. Scott-James. I had covered all the ground in my lecture during my preparations for a book I published some time ago, and took up *The Making of Literature* only a few hours before my lecture, and I stood amazed at the brilliance of this work, which is not only completely at home in the material, but has the finest tact in dealing with it. I found that wherever I had used material that he had not (other than specific book reviews, such as Dr. Johnson's *Lives of the Poets* or Hazlitt's *Spirit of the Age*), I was always wrong. I had intended to quote Schiller's correspondence on the subject of art but I did not, and found when the time came it was too fussy and intricate to use for anybody who has not a ground plan of literary criticism in his mind. He also omits a great many gods of the text-books who are not gods at all. For example, he does not repeat the preposterous legend that there is material of value relevant to this subject in *Wilhelm Meister*: or the equally unfounded allegation that G. H. Lewes was a critic of parts. It does not seem to me that the reviews have laid stress on the importance of this book, which is the only attempt I know to collate this unwieldy body of material. I assure every teacher or writer that it is a work which ought to be acquired at any cost.

EXPERIMENT IN CRITICISM

By T. S. ELIOT

THERE is no department of literature in which it is more difficult to establish a distinction between 'traditional' and 'experimental' work than literary criticism. For here both words may be taken in two senses. By traditional criticism we may mean that which follows the same methods, aims at the same ends, and expresses much the same state of mind as the criticism of the preceding generation. Or we may mean something quite different: a criticism which has a definite theory of the meaning and value of the term 'tradition', and which may be experimental in reverting to masters who have been forgotten. And as for 'experiment' one may mean the more original work of the present generation, or else the work of critics who are pushing into new fields of inquiry, or enlarging the scope of criticism with other kinds of knowledge. To use the word 'experimental' in the first sense would be invidious, for it would cover all the critical work of our time which one considers to have merit. For it is obvious that every generation has a new point of view, and is self-conscious in the critic; his work is twofold, to interpret the past to the present, and to judge the present in the light of the past. We have to see literature through our own temperament in order to see it at all, though our vision is always partial and our judgement always prejudiced; no generation, and no individual, can appreciate *every* dead author and every past period; universal good taste is never realized. In this way, all criticism is experimental, just as the mode of life of every generation is an experiment. It is

only in my second sense, therefore, that it is worth while
to talk of experimental criticism; only by considering
what critics to-day may be *deliberately* attempting some
kind of critical work which has not been deliberately
attempted before.

In order to make clear exactly what there is that is
new in contemporary critical writing I shall have to go
back a hundred years. We may say, roughly, that
modern criticism begins with the work of the French
critic Sainte-Beuve, that is to say about the year 1826.
Before him, Coleridge had attempted a new type of
criticism, a type which is in some respects more allied
to what is now called aesthetics than to literary criticism.
But from the Renaissance through the eighteenth century
literary criticism had been confined to two narrow and
closely related types. One was a type which has always
existed and I hope always will; for it can always have
very great value: it may be called practical notes on the
art of writing by practitioners, parallel to the treatises on
painting which have been left us by Leonardo da Vinci
and others. Such notes are of the greatest value to other
artists, particularly when studied in conjunction with
the author's own work. Two classical examples in
English are the Elizabethan treatises on rhymed and
unrhymed verse written by Thomas Campion and
Samuel Daniel. The prefaces and essays of Dryden, the
prefaces of Corneille, are of the same type but on a
larger scale and engage wider issues. But at the same
time there is a large body of criticism, a considerable
quantity in English and still more in French, written
by men who were professionally critics rather than
creative writers: the most famous critic of this sort is of
course Boileau. This type of critic was primarily the

arbiter of taste, and his task was to praise and condemn the work of his contemporaries, and especially to lay down the laws of good writing. These laws were supposed to be drawn from the practice, but still more from the theory, of the ancients. Aristotle was highly respected; but in practice this type of criticism was usually far from following the profound insight of Aristotle, and confined itself to translating, imitating, and plagiarizing Horace's *Art of Poetry*. At its best, it confirmed and maintained permanent standards of good writing; at its worst it was a mere sequence of precepts. In general, French criticism was more theoretic, and as in La Harpe, more desiccated; the normal English type was nearer to plain good sense, as in Johnson's *Lives of the Poets;* though interesting theory, usually on specific literary types such as the drama, is found in authors like Thomas Rymer and Daniel Webb in the seventeenth and eighteenth centuries.

It is worth delaying for a moment to point out one of the qualities of seventeenth- and eighteenth-century literary criticism, which gives it enduring value and at the same time marks it off from more modern criticism. We are apt to think of this older criticism as dry and formal, and as setting up classical moulds in which no living literature could be shaped. But we should remember in its favour that this criticism recognized literature as literature, and not another thing. Literature was something distinct from philosophy and psychology and every other study; and its purpose was to give a refined pleasure to persons of sufficient leisure and breeding. If the older critics had not taken for granted that literature was something primarily to be enjoyed, they could not have occupied themselves so sedulously with laying down rules of what was right to enjoy. This seems a very commonplace remark, and no distinction; but if you compare the criticism of those two centuries with that of the nineteenth, you will see that the latter does not take this simple truth wholly for granted. Literature is often treated by the critic rather as a means for eliciting truth or acquiring knowledge. If the critic is of a more philosophic or religious mind, he will look for the expression of philosophic or religious intuition in the work of the author criticized; if he is of a more realistic turn, he will look to literature as material for the discovery of psychological truths, or as documents illustrating social history. Even in the mouths of Walter Pater and his disciples, the phrase 'art for art's sake' means something very different from the sense in which literature was literature for literature's sake up to the latter part of the eighteenth century. If you read carefully the famous epilogue to Pater's *Studies in the Renaissance* you will see that 'art for art's sake' means nothing less than art as a substitute for everything else, and as a purveyor of emotions and sensations which belong to life rather than to art. To distinguish clearly between these two attitudes, that of art for art's sake and that of the eighteenth century, does require a strong effort of imagination. But the former doctrine would have been unintelligible to the earlier age. For the earlier period, art and literature were not substitutes for religion or philosophy or morals or politics, any more than for duelling or love-making: they were special and limited adornments of life. On each side there is a profit and a loss. We have gained perhaps a deeper insight, now and then; whether we enjoy literature any more keenly than our ancestors I do not know; but I think we should

return again and again to the critical writings of the
seventeenth and eighteenth centuries, to remind ourselves of that simple truth that literature is primarily
literature, a means of refined and intellectual pleasure.

How, we ask immediately, did human beings ever
come to abandon so simple and satisfying a limitation
of criticism? The change comes about incidentally to
a larger change, which may be described as the growth
of the *historical* attitude. But this change—to which I
shall return in a moment—is preceded, so far as literary
criticism is concerned—by a freakish phenomenon, by
a book written by one of the wisest and most foolish men
of his time and perhaps the most extraordinary; a book
which is itself one of the wisest and silliest, the most
exciting and most exasperating books of criticism ever
written—the *Biographia Literaria* of Coleridge. There, if
you like, was 'experiment in criticism', everything in
fact except the power of sticking to the point—a power
noticeably absent from Coleridge's ill-regulated life.
Coleridge was one of the most learned men of his time,
and no man of his time had wider interests except
Goethe; and one of the first things that strikes us about
his book, besides its uncommon diffuseness, is the novel
variety of knowledge which he brings to bear on literary
criticism. Much of his knowledge, as of the romantic
German philosophers, does not seem to us to-day
particularly worth having, but it was held to be valuable
then; and we owe to Coleridge as much as to anybody
our enjoyment of the doubtful benefits of German
Idealism. His book naturally contains specimens of
several types of criticism; its impulse, of course, was a
defence of the new—or as the newspapers of our time
would say, 'modernist' poetry of Wordsworth; and as

such belongs to the type of technical notes of a craftsman; but when Coleridge started on anything, it could lead to almost everything else. He had not the historical point of view, but by the catholicity of his literary lore, and his ability for sudden and illuminating comparisons drawn from poetry of different ages and different languages, he anticipated some of the most useful accomplishments of the historical method. But one thing that Coleridge did effect for literary criticism is this. He brought out clearly the relation of literary criticism to that branch of philosophy which has flourished amazingly under the name of aesthetics; and, following German writers whom he had studied, he puts the criticism of literature in its place as merely one department of the theoretic study of the Fine Arts in general. His fine discrimination of Fancy and Imagination cannot be held as permanent, for terms and relations change; but it remains one of the important texts for all who would consider the nature of poetic imagination. And he establishes literary criticism as a part of philosophy: or, to put it more moderately, he made it necessary for the 'literary critic' to acquaint himself with general philosophy and metaphysics.

Biographia Literaria appeared in 1817; the activities of Charles Augustin Sainte-Beuve may be said to begin about 1826. Coleridge and Sainte-Beuve have very little in common, as little, that is, as two men who were both great critics could have in common. And Sainte-Beuve would not have been a great critic solely on the ground of what is new and experimental in his work. He had a very French intelligence and good taste which enabled him to share the ideals and sympathies of the great French writers of every time; there was much in

him of the eighteenth century, a good deal even of the
seventeenth. There were many gaps, certainly, in his
appreciations, both of his contemporaries and of his
predecessors; but he had that essential critical quality
of imagination which made it possible for him to grasp
literature as a whole. Where he differed from previous
French critics was in his implicit conception of literature,
not only as a body of writings to be enjoyed, but as a
process of change in history, and as a part of the study
of history. The notion that literary values are relative
to literary periods, that the literature of a period is
primarily an expression and a symptom of the time, is
so natural to us now that we can hardly detach our
minds from it. We can hardly conceive that the degree
and kind of self-consciousness which we have could ever
not have been. How much criticism of contemporary
literature is taken up with discussing whether, and in
what degree, this book or novel or poem is expressive
of *our* mentality, of the personality of *our* age; and how
often our critics seem to be interested rather in in-
quiring what *we* (including themselves) are like, than
with the book, novel, or poem as a work of art! This
is an extreme, but the extreme of a tendency which
began, in criticism, a good hundred years ago. Sainte-
Beuve was not, like Coleridge, a metaphysician; he is
indeed more modern and more sceptical; but he was
the first interesting historian in criticism. And it is by
no means irrelevant that he began his career with the
study of medicine; he is not only an historian but a
biologist in criticism.

It is, I think, interesting to turn to some good recent
piece of literary criticism, and underline some of the
assumptions of knowledge and theory which you would

not find in criticism of two hundred years ago. Mr. Herbert Read's lucid little primer, *Phases of English Poetry*, will do for our purpose. On the second page he tells us that his is an inquiry into the *evolution* of poetry, and speaks presently of English poetry as a 'living and developing organism'. Even these few words should give a hint of the extent to which the critical apparatus has changed with the general changes in scientific and historical conceptions, when a literary critic can treat his audience to terms like 'evolution' and 'living organism' with the assurance of their being immediately apprehended. He is taking for granted certain vague but universal biological ideas. A little later he informs us that 'the beginning of this study belongs to anthropology'. Now, a great deal of work has had to be done by a great many people, and already more or less popularized, before a critic of literature can talk in this way. The work of Bastian, Tylor, Mannhardt, Durkheim, Levy-Bruhl, Frazer, Miss Harrison, and many others has gone before. And a great deal of purely literary investigation has been made too, before any one can talk of the evolution of poetry. Mr. Read begins by studying the origins of ballad poetry. It would not have been possible for him to do so without a great deal of work done in the later nineteenth century and the early twentieth; for example, by Professor Child of Harvard, Professor Gommere of Haverford, Professor Gaston Paris of the Sorbonne, and Professor W. P. Ker of London. Such studies in ballad poetry, and in all the heretofore unexplored ages of literature, have fostered in us the sense of flux and evolution, the sense of the relation of the poetry of each period to the civilization of the period, and also have tended slightly to *level* literary values. It was W. P. Ker, who perhaps knew the whole history of European poetry better than any man of his time, who said that in literature there were no Dark Ages. And in the next paragraph to the one which I have just quoted, Mr. Read observes that in theories of the origin of poetry we 'go right back to the origin of speech'. Even to make so simple a remark as this requires the work of another group of scientists: the philologists. The modern critic must have some acquaintance with them too—with the work of such contemporary philologists as Professor Jespersen of Copenhagen.

There are other branches of knowledge (or at least of science) some acquaintance with which you take for granted in any applicant whom you may employ as literary critic. Especially of course psychology, particularly analytical psychology. All of the studies I have mentioned, and more, do themselves touch the edges, and handle some of the problems, of criticism; so conversely the critic has to know something about them. The modern critic is distinguished first by the current notions which he shares with all educated or half-educated persons, such as the notion of evolution, and by the number and variety of sciences of which he has to know a little. And he has to know them, not in order to do their work for them, but to collaborate— and also, in order that he may know where to stop. We require much general knowledge in order to see the limits of our particular ignorance.

Now although Sainte-Beuve did not have the equipment which we expect of our contemporaries, he had a great deal of the method, and very typically the state of mind which results from such a method at our stage of history. The awareness of the process of time has obscured the frontiers between literature and everything else. If you read the earlier critics, such as Dryden, you find the problems of literature comparatively simple ones. For Dryden and his contemporaries there were the Greek and Latin classics, a solid block of accepted canon, and there were their contemporaries, that is to say, English literature from Shakespeare and French literature from Malherbe; and they spent a good deal of their time in discussing whether the moderns, as they called themselves, had any literary virtues not surpassed by the ancients. Their estimate of the classics was not complicated by worrying about serpent and mistletoe cults, or the finances of the Athenian government. And between the ancients and Shakespeare and Malherbe there was nothing much to think about. They had really a great deal more faith in themselves than we have. They were certainly not bothered about 'the future'. It often seems to me that all our concern about the future, and even the most optimistic visions of it which Mr. Shaw and Mr. Wells used to enjoy, are tokens of a profound pessimism. We hardly have time to get any fun out of what is being written now, so concerned are we about the quality of what may be written fifty years hence. Even Mr. Read's chapter on 'Modern Poetry' seems to be as much engrossed by the puzzle of what poetry will be as by the puzzle of what it is. This kind of doubt seems to me to continue the doubt of Sainte-Beuve and Renan. Sainte-Beuve wrote a book of seven volumes on that remarkable French religious movement of the seventeenth century known as *Port Royal*, and on that remarkable group of religious people of whom the most famous is Pascal. It is the masterpiece on that subject. It comes to no conclusion. It ends with the words;

'He who had it most at heart to know his object, whose ambition was most engaged in seizing it, whose pride was most alert to paint it—how powerless he feels, and how far beneath his task, on the day when, seeing it almost finished and the result obtained, he feels his exaltation sink, feels himself overcome by faintness and inevitable disgust, and perceives in his turn that he too is only a fleeting illusion in the midst of the infinite illusory flux!'

Sainte-Beuve was a modern critic for this reason: he was a man of restless curiosity about life, society, civilization, and all the problems which the study of history arouses. He studied these things *through* literature, because that was the centre of his interests; and he never lost his literary sensibility in his investigation of problems reaching far beyond literature. But he was an historian, a sociologist (in the best sense of that word) and a moralist. He is a typical modern critic in that he found himself obliged to brood over the larger and darker problems which, in the modern world, lie behind the specific problems of literature.

The criticism of literature has by no means been absorbed in something else, as alchemy into chemistry. The core of the matter is still there, though the ramifications are endless, and the task of the critic is indeed hard. But there is still a valid distinction to be drawn between those modern critics who would make literature a *substitute* for a definite philosophy and theology, and thus promulgate, in an inverted form, the old gospel of art for art's sake, and those who would try to keep the distinctions clear, while admitting that the study of the one leads to the other, and that the possession of clear literary standards must imply the possession of clear moral standards. The various attempts to find the fundamental axioms behind both good literature and good life are among the most interesting 'experiments' of criticism in our time.

The most considerable of such attempts so far is that which is known under the name of Humanism, and which owes its origin chiefly to the work of Professor Babbitt of Harvard. Mr. Babbitt, who is one of the most learned men of our time, is to some extent a disciple of Sainte-Beuve. There is no one living who knows more intimately (among many other things) the whole history of literary criticism. In his own writings, still more positively than in those of Sainte-Beuve, the criticism of literature has been a means of criticizing every aspect of modern society. He is a scholar of classical education and classical tastes. He is keenly aware of the fact that the weaknesses of modern literature are symptoms of the weaknesses of modern civilization, and he has set himself with immense patience and perseverance to analyse these weaknesses. His conclusions may be read in his two most recent books, *Rousseau and Romanticism*, an account and a theory of the deterioration of taste since the early eighteenth century, and a book of still wider scope, *Democracy and Leadership*. As a moralist and as an Anglo-Saxon, he has on one side more in common with Matthew Arnold than with Sainte-Beuve. The tendency of the 'humanist' in France is rather to diagnose without prescribing a remedy; witness two recent books of brilliant literary and social criticism by M. Julien Benda, *Belphégor* and *La Trahison des Clercs;* the Anglo-Saxon finds it intolerable to diagnose a disease without prescribing a remedy.

P

Mr. Babbitt, like Arnold and Sainte-Beuve, finds that the decay of religious dogma has inflicted grave injury on society; like Arnold and Sainte-Beuve, he refuses to accept the remedy of returning to religious dogma; like Arnold and unlike Sainte-Beuve, he proposes another remedy, a theory of positive ethics based on human experiment, on the needs and capacities of the human as human, without reference to revelation or to supernatural authority or aid.

I do not propose, in this brief account, to discuss Mr. Babbitt's positive contribution, or the points at which I agree or disagree. I only want to call attention to a most important movement which is primarily, or in its inception, a movement within literary criticism, and of which a great deal more will be heard. It is significant because it shows that the modern literary critic must be an 'experimenter' outside of what you might at first consider his own province; and as evidence that nowadays there is no literary problem which does not lead us irresistibly to larger problems. There is one weakness, or rather danger, of literary criticism which perceives the inevitable continuation of literary questions into general questions, which I might as well point out, because otherwise you will see it for yourselves and attach too much importance to it. The danger is that when a critic has grasped these vital moral problems which rise out of literary criticism, he may lose his detachment and submerge his sensibility. He may become too much a servant of his mind and conscience; he may be too impatient with contemporary literature, having pigeonholed it under one or another of the modern social maladies; and may demand edification at once, when appreciation of genius and accomplishment should come first. When he upholds 'classicism' and denounces 'romanticism' he is likely to give the impression that we should write like Sophocles or Racine: that everything contemporary is 'romantic' and therefore not worth talking about. He makes us suspect that if a truly great, original classical work of imagination were to be written to-day, no one would like it. There will always be romantic people to admire romantic work; but we wonder whether the classicists would certainly know a classical work when it came. But these qualifications should not lead us to reject the humanist's theories: they should only lead us to apply them for ourselves.

Mr. Ramon Fernandez is a younger critic, who has also taken the word Humanism for his device, though his humanism, arrived at independently in France, is of a rather different brand from that which has arisen in America. His humanism has this in common: that it is also a development from literary criticism, and that it is also an attempt to arrive at a positive system of ethics while rejecting any revealed religion or supernatural authority. His first volume of essays, *Messages*, has been translated into English (Cape): it is important, I think, not so much by its achievement—for indeed the author has still a great many tangled knots in his style, which is cumbered by a good deal of philosophical and psychological terminology—as by its new attempt. Mr. Fernandez is less encyclopaedic, less concerned with the past. He pores steadily over contemporaries and over the nineteenth century, and is more devoted to the study of special individuals, such as Montaigne, than to the study of the general course of literary history. Like the American humanists, he ponders over 'classicism' and 'romanticism'; but he wishes to be flexible, and is anxious to distinguish the essentials of classicism (which he finds, for instance, in George Eliot) from its appearances at any particular time. His theory is one which I do not wholly understand, and which has not yet been fully expounded, and probably not yet fully developed: but he illustrates, as clearly as the American humanists, the new experimental method of dealing with literary problems as moral problems, and the attempt to find guidance in conduct out of statement in literature—especially from the great novelists, and particularly, for he is a close student of English literature, from George Eliot and George Meredith. (In any case, his essay on Marcel Proust, the French novelist, in the volume mentioned, is a masterpiece of his particular method.) He is, in general, less the sociologist and more the individual psychologist. And from the best of his essays on novelists one draws this conclusion: that if we should exclude from literary criticism all but purely literary considerations, there would not only be very little to talk about, but actually we should be left without even literary appreciation. This is true of our appreciation of ancient authors, but still more obviously of our appreciation of modern authors. For the same expansion of interest which has been imposed upon the modern critic has been imposed, or at least has been assumed, by the modern imaginative writer. We cannot write a purely literary criticism of George Eliot, for instance, unless it is admittedly a very imperfect criticism: for as the interests of the author were wide, so must be those of the critic.

I have tried to show that the tendency throughout a whole epoch to the present moment has been to widen the scope of criticism and increase the demands made upon the critic. This development might be traced in terms of the development of human self-consciousness, but that is a general philosophical question beyond the margin of this lecture. There is along with this expansion a compensating tendency. As the number of sciences multiply, of sciences that is which have a bearing upon criticism, so we ask ourselves first whether there is still any justification for literary criticism at all, or whether we should not merely allow the subject to be absorbed gently into exacter sciences which will each annex some side of criticism. Just as in the history of philosophy, we find many subjects surrendered from time to time by philosophy, now to mathematics and physics, now to biology and psychology; until there seems to be almost nothing left to philosophize about. I think that the answer is clear: that so long as literature is literature, so long will there be a place for criticism of it, for criticism, that is, on the same basis as that on which the literature itself is made. For so long as poetry and fiction and such things are written, its first purpose must always be what it always has been—to give a peculiar kind of pleasure which has something constant in it throughout the ages, however difficult and various our explanations of that pleasure may be. The task of criticism will be, accordingly, not only to expand its borders but to clarify its centre, and the insistency of the latter need grows with that of the former. Two hundred years ago, when it was taken for granted that one knew well enough what literature was, and it was not the number of other things which it is always now seeming to be, terms could be used more freely and carelessly without close definition. Now, there is an urgent need for experiment in criticism of a new kind, which will consist largely in a logical and dialectical study of the terms used. My own interest in these problems has been fostered partly by dissatisfaction with the *meaning* of my own statements in criticism, and partly by dissatisfaction with the terminology of the Humanists. In literary criticism we are constantly using terms which we cannot define, and defining other things by them. We are constantly using terms which have an *in*tension and an *ex*tension which do not quite fit; theoretically they ought to be made to fit; but if they cannot, then some other way must be found of dealing with them so that we may know at every moment what we mean. I will take a very simple example with which I have been dealing myself: the possibility of defining 'metaphysical poetry'. Here is a term which has a whole history of meanings down to the present time, all of which must be recognized, although it cannot have all of them at once. The term means, on the one hand, a certain group of English poets in the seventeenth century. On the other hand, it must have an intensive meaning, must stand for a peculiar whole of qualities which is exemplified by the several poets. The ordinary critical method would be to define what 'metaphysical poetry' means to you in the abstract, fit as many poets to it as well as you can, and reject the rest. Or else, you take the poets who have been held to be 'metaphysical', and find out what they have in common. The odd thing is that by doing the sum, so to speak, in two different ways, you get two different results. A larger problem in the same kind of definition is that of Classicism and Romanticism. Every one who writes about these two abstractions believes that he knows what the words mean; actually they mean something a little different for each observer, and merely mean to mean the same things. In this way you have material for endless wrangling with no conclusion, which is not satisfactory. Such problems involve, of course, both logic and the theory of knowledge and psychology; there is no one, perhaps, more concerned with them than Mr. I. A. Richards, the author of *Principles of Literary Criticism* and *Practical Criticism*.

There is good cause for believing—apart from the obvious assertion that every generation must criticize for itself—that literary criticism, far from being exhausted, has hardly begun its work. On the other hand, I am more than sceptical of the old superstition that criticism and 'creative writing' never flourish in the same age: that is a generalization drawn from a superficial inspection of some past ages. 'Creative writing' can look after itself; and certainly it will be none the better for suppressing the critical curiosity. And in any case, the times which we have lived in seem to me, on the false antithesis mentioned, rather 'creative' than 'critical'. (The current superstition that our epoch is Alexandrine, decadent, or 'disillusioned' is parallel; there are no 'disillusioned ages', only disillusioned individuals; and our time is just as deluded as any other.) The present age has been, rather, uncritical, and partly for economic causes. The 'critic' has been chiefly the reviewer, that is to say, the hurried amateur wage-slave. I am aware of the danger that the types of criticism in which I am interested may become too professional and technical. What I hope for is the collaboration of critics of various special training, and perhaps the pooling and sorting of their contributions by men who will be neither specialists nor amateurs.

THE CITY LITERARY INSTITUTE

Goldsmith Street, Drury Lane, London, W.C. 2.

THE Institute is an Adult Educational Centre maintained as part of the provision for part-time education by the London County Council. The curriculum is based upon the humanities; and the courses, which are devised on broadly cultural lines, include the study of Literature and Language, Art, Speech and Drama, Music and Dancing, Philosophy and Natural Science, Economics, Social and Political Theory, History and Biography, Travel and Folk-lore. Ordinarily, each study group meets for lecture and discussion or practice weekly throughout the academic year.

The London County Council accepts no responsibility for any opinions or conclusions expressed in this volume.

PRINTED IN GREAT BRITAIN AT THE UNIVERSITY PRESS, OXFORD
BY JOHN JOHNSON, PRINTER TO THE UNIVERSITY